THE DRIFTING HOME

BY

ERNEST R. GROVES

Professor of Sociology, Boston University
Author of 'Personality and Social Adjustment' and 'Social
Problems and Education'; co-author of 'Wholesome Childhood'

BOSTON AND NEW YORK

HOUGHTON MIFFLIN COMPANY

The Riverside Press Cambridge

1926

The Riverside Press
CAMBRIDGE · MASSACHUSETTS
PRINTED IN THE U.S.A.

TO MY AUNT

ETTA L. BARKER

FROM EARLY CHILDHOOD

MY OTHER MOTHER

PREFACE

THERE is in this country a widespread and increasing interest in better homes, showing itself in many forms and expressing the conviction of individuals and organizations that we have in America both the need and the opportunity of improving home life. This is one of the happy facts of our present social trends, the promise of a family equal to the demands put upon it by modern life. Thoughtful men and women everywhere are in sympathy with the emphasis being placed upon the necessity of preventing the American family from falling to low standards.

It is not just to the actual facts to consider the problems of the family as something apart from our larger social situation. Neither is it a fair interpretation of the family to forget the multitude of successful homes which in my opinion far outnumber those that by their failure attract attention.

This book treats some of the outstanding social problems of the home, but without pessimism as to the future of the home and, I trust, without exaggeration of its present needs. It aims to contribute to the growing belief that education must in some form undertake the task of constructing the better home of the future.

Some of the chapters have already appeared in magazines and I thank the editors of the various periodicals for the opportunity of presenting this material: part of 'The Drifting Home,' in 'The Christian Advocate'; 'Social Influences Affecting Family Life,' in the 'American Journal of Sociology'; part of 'The Home a Human Need,' in 'The World To-morrow,' and 'Parents Who Haven't Grown Up,' in 'Harper's Monthly.'

I desire to express my appreciation of the help given me in the preparation of this book by my wife, Gladys Hoagland Groves.

E. R. G.

CONTENTS

THE DRIFTING HOME

.:.

CHAPTER I

THE DRIFTING HOME

THERE are three kinds of American homes, the good, bad, and bewildered. There have always been good and bad homes. The difference is that now our good homes are better than they have ever been in the past, and our bad homes are more of a menace than they have ever been. This is because the conditions of social life to-day give the good home more opportunity for its wholesome service, while intensifying the failure of the bad home. Modern life necessarily puts a heavier task upon the family and as a consequence it either achieves successes unattainable in the past or shows by a perverted use of the resources of our present way of living how much social evil can flow out of the bad home.

From the beginning there have been good

homes and bad homes, but as a characteristic type of family life the bewildered home is something new. For this reason we must consider the third type of family peculiarly representative of the social life that now is.

This drifting home has been torn from its anchorage in the elemental needs of human nature by the swiftly running current of modern civilization. All family life is undergoing change, for this is the period of transition; but the family which has been sent adrift is not merely perplexed, it is literally bewildered; it senses the loss of old landmarks even though it tries to find security in traditions that crumble at its touch.

No one who thinks at all of the plight of the present-day bewildered home is surprised that it is in trouble; the only wonder is that it is not in more serious difficulty. The family has certainly been neglected. This shows itself when we separate the two parts of the home, its home-making and its housekeeping. Housekeeping, fortunately, has been simplified and to some extent farmed out. In the cities it has been reduced to a very small proportion. On the whole, however, it still occupies the larger amount of time spent in the home by the wife and mother. The great majority of women in charge of homes have found that there is a point beyond which the work of housekeeping cannot be reduced without risking the existence of the home itself. When we turn to the home-making part, we find the situation very different. Here the woman's contribution is to a large extent a matter of choice; she can, if she pleases, almost entirely neglect this part of her home task, especially after her children have reached the age at which they can be rushed to school. A good part of the leisure women now enjoy has come from their reducing the amount of time spent with their children or in dealing with the problems of association that naturally arise in a home.

If the mother has been negligent at this point, what must be said of the father? When one catalogues the fathers of one's acquaintance, one soon discovers how few of them give influence or time to their home. Indeed, a code of behavior has become acceptable which requires mostly of the father that he be kind and a good provider; as long as he keeps the pocketbook replenished, he is regarded as having met his obligations. Yet it is obvious that there can be no home in the historic sense of home if the mother limits her responsibilities to housekeeping and the father his to the making of the family income.

As a rule family failure is not erupted with volcanic suddenness, but creeps forward slowly and reveals itself little by little. Gradually the parent begins to realize that something is going wrong; the children are neither happy nor safely prepared to meet life. In a great number of cases the children were not wanted and the parents have neglected them as much as possible in their search for happiness. This policy frees husband and wife from innumerable responsibilities; they have invested the time saved in business, social trivialities, pleasures, and occasionally in useful forms of public service. Those who have shirked their duties toward their children do not appear to have found greater happiness in their more abundant leisure. Some discover this only when it is tragically too late; others never stop long enough in their pleasure hunt to recognize their misstep.

It is clear that there are elements in our civilization that easily blight family life. No elaborate analysis is necessary to reveal what these influences are: although found in myriad forms they boil down to competition, luxury, and lack of preparation for home life. Competition has been man's indispensable stimulus; it has pushed him forward, driven him over obstacles that appeared insurmountable. Competition easily becomes a cruel tyrant that keeps men too busy struggling to win their goals to enjoy the game of life which they play. The situation is not much better for the hordes of people whose ambition has been sapped by treadmill occupations, but who without any sense of achievement are prodded by economic pressure, the instrument by which the most competitive keep the industrial world at its mad pace. Neither those who direct competition nor those who feel its force have inclination or time to consider family welfare.

'Surely you are not forgetting the enormous increase in leisure made possible by modern industry?' asks the discriminating reader. No, indeed; but what modern life has given us is not leisure, but its possibility.

He who never catches up with time or struggles to keep the pace set by a machine geared to the maximum production until all vitality evaporates cannot accurately be described as enjoying leisure. Fortunately a great multitude refuse to be victimized by an industrial system that is a good human servant but a miserable taskmaster, and from such come our good homes.

Frequently the bewildered home has been led astray by its craving for luxury. Luxury, of course, is in a sense relative. Although in abundance and quality modern luxuries still observe class distinctions, one of the profound facts of present-day culture is the democratizing of the desire for luxuries; we find it in all classes, proportionately intense for those who have little and those who have much. It is an inspiring prophecy that the longing for material satisfactions should be not only so widespread but increasingly capable of attaining its ends.

There are luxuries that minister to home enjoyments and if they are obtained by sacrifice the experience only cements more firmly the affection of the various members; there are also luxuries that clog family life, distort true values, and even strip the family of necessities that it requires for its own comfort and security. Many a family has gone adrift in its quest for unwise luxuries.

Luxury most commonly attacks the family life by crushing its sympathies, turning the attention of its members from their more satisfying and abiding resources to the noisy and ostentatious luxuries flaunted by the grasping advertiser, which have been elevated by social suggestion until they assume the size of an absolute necessity. It is folly to try to entice man to return to the simple life, but if the home is to have a fair chance education must with seriousness attempt to prepare man to lead a more comfortable and discriminating life.

It is not only the bewildered family that is adrift. Civilization itself has departed from its moorings. Taxation, education, the practical everyday ethics that constitute man's actual morality, and other basic forms of culture are slipping away from concern for the prosperity of the home. Many of those who make our laws, manage our businesses, produce the thoughts that influence action, are themselves destitute of family interests and naturally equally indifferent to the family needs of others. They do not attack the family so much as neglect it, but the family is as easily hurt by flank as by frontal attack. Legislation that forgets the family can as deeply hurt it, for example, by influencing the birth rate or the marriage rate or not guarding the death rate, as if the law were passed by malignant intent. In the same way education or industry or public opinion or practical ethics may, by merely forgetting to consider its effect upon family life, become an enemy of the home.

The drifting home is unlike the bad home in its power of recovery; it can be brought back to safe anchorage. More important still, such homes can easily be prevented. If they were destitute of right purposes they would not be so bewildered, but like the bad home they would take their faults for granted.

What the perplexed home needs more than anything else is insight into the nature of its difficulties. It is a victim of the changing conditions of modern life, of the very culture that man by centuries of achievement has finally attained. Behind the social conditions that the perplexed parent regards with suspicion because he realizes that his home is adrift is science, the creator of the everyday world of modern man. It is to this apparent mischief-maker that the parent must go for interpretation of the problems he meets and assistance in handling them. Naturally he hesitates to seek help from the apparent source of so much of his trouble. What he does not see is that it is unbalanced science that is raising havoc with our homes; the fault is not alone that of material science which has leaped forward from success to success until it has already given to man resources beyond his former dreams, but of the belated science of human behavior that has lagged behind. Now that we are beginning to have a scientific understanding of human behavior, we must make use of it; we must especially bring it to parents that they may have its advantage in making the delicate adjustments of modern home life.

Neither the thirst for fad nor the desire to crusade is behind the growing insistence that education seriously consider its obligations to parents and to homes; this demand is simply the logical expression of a great human need. If experience, interpreted with the impartiality of science, can reveal principles of behavior that explain the meaning of the crises that arise in family associations and bring out the inherent dangers as well as the values of the home, then here is a body of knowledge that people want and if education falters at this point its successes elsewhere will only hamper the home all the more. It is useless to try to meet the problems of the present home with the equipment of yesterday. Our fathers neither had this scientific help nor had such need of it. Each generation builds up the means by which it protects itself against the risks that come from the ongoing of human culture. Homemakers need training, and fortunately resources are at hand to meet their need. It is not just a matter of science, but the program that leaves science out is hopeless. The ideas of modern life must be more and more those that emphasize home values, but without science to disclose the means, the demands for more normal standards will get nowhere. Higher standards of family life we must have, for even civilization cannot be secure if too many homes get adrift. If one takes this to heart he is not likely to have misgivings. The social need of better homes must force a reaction from that neglect of family values which in the recent past has been so widespread both in our thinking and our conduct.

One might think that anyone who knew at all the predicament in which the modern American parent finds himself would welcome the effort to bring science to the assistance of the home. But the fact is that even professional social workers have expressed skepticism when asked to coöperate in the effort to bring to parents scientific knowledge of practical value. A common expression of this sentiment is, ' The only thing the matter with the home is the selfishness of the people in it, and what can science do to help that?' But selfishness is merely a label of attitude or habits, the origin of which science is even now able to untangle. He who has really studied family problems realizes also that what is commonly called unselfishness is not infrequently the stumbling block in the way of wholesome family life. The unselfish mother may, through lack of judgment or restraint, produce a spoiled or infantile personality in her grown-up child just as surely as an ignorant but well-intentioned cook may ruin the dinner.

The opposition to the use of science as an aid to men and women who face the problems of marriage and parenthood is rapidly passing, the need of such help from science is so obvious and so desperate. The situation will invite the fakir who always has his eye open for new ways of getting an easy living. The cautious scientist will be surprised to find going through the opening he has made in the indifference or despair of the home his enemy the charlatan of oily tongue, ever ready to capitalize an opportunity when the crust of tradition breaks.

It is of course the thoughtful and conscientious parent who most feels the need of having scientific help in meeting his problems of child-training. In the long run this will prove fortunate for it will prevent the movement to educate parents from acquiring any tinge of charitable stigma. At present those in greatest difficulty do not realize the serious character of their mistakes in dealing with their children, nor do they know of the sources of possible help. This condition will soon change, for the necessity of providing special training for parents is being recognized by different kinds of organizations and educational institutions.

Science is now ready to serve the home. This fact must not tempt those interested in helping family life by making use of recent information gathered by psychology and sociology to claim too much for the new knowledge. Only a beginning has been made in the collection of well-tested facts regarding child-training and home reactions. What we have is most useful but it is neither adequate nor does it promise forthcoming information that will be so satisfactory as to be all-sufficient.

There must be, however, no misunderstanding as to what is involved in preparation for parenthood. We cannot get much better mothers and fathers than we now have if we attempt merely to teach them an improved technique in dealing with their children. Nothing short of growth in parental character will get the bewildered home out of its present difficulties. The teaching of parents must get down to bed-rock motives and apply the leverage of affection, moral obligation and religious inspiration. Parents need more incentive as well as greater insight.

When science is applied to human relations it has to adapt itself to human qualities, it cannot be merely cold fact or mechanical processes; it requires interpretation by winsome teachers who have the natural gifts of persuasive leadership. The investigator is not always a skilful advocate: both types of persons have their part in the task of educating parents and the newly married. The success of the rapidly developing program for adult education will depend upon the harmonious working together of the mature, well trained investigator and the skilful teacher. At last education has reached the parent. Now we want information of practical value in meeting actual home situations and popular instructors who can make the facts clear and compelling. Nothing has happened in recent years of greater promise for home life than the swiftly developing idea that if society is to have good parents it must train them. *Laissez faire* in home-making is at last near its end.

CHAPTER II

SOCIAL INFLUENCES AFFECTING HOME LIFE

THE home is changing. This is the most significant fact regarding the home, and perhaps the most important fact in our current civilization. There can be no doubt as to the cause of the changes taking place with reference to the home. Social life outside the home has changed, mostly due to science and the greater intellectual freedom that follows closely after science. The home has felt these outside conditions and in turn has been forced to modify former habits and motives.

It is not easy, however, to discover the full meaning of these changes in the home. Some are obvious and much talked about. These, perhaps, are on the surface, but on that account they are not necessarily less serious in their import. On the other hand, they may be the expression of deeply hidden causes, much more difficult to detect. Science cannot, of course, have the assistance of experiment in uncovering the character of contemporaneous home life. In its observations it is hampered by the sense of intimacy, the social reticence, and even outward deceit, which make a collecting of home experiences unusually difficult and bare statistics misleading.

No progress can be made in an analysis of modern home life unless it be clearly kept in mind that we place together two things in our ordinary discussion of the home: one is marriage and the other is parenthood. These two parts of home life are both changing, but the results are not the same. Each feels the sweep of modern life, for the influences that strike the one also beat against the other.

The social influences that operate upon marriage and parenthood are not special and peculiar, but everyday affairs. They come out of the commonplace experiences of average men and women. If they are hard to separate and classify, it is because their perpetual presence dulls our attention, while our own emotional reactions to them make it hard for us to consider them objectively.

The social forces are not orderly in their

movement upon the home. They do not act in harmony nor with the certainty of natural law. They crash in discord, and their influence differs as they penetrate individual homes. Nevertheless they are ever present, and no family that has any contact with modern civilization escapes making some response.

The home is a more sensitive social institution than we are wont to think. Sentiment often misreads a home situation and covers up the great differences between a generation and the one preceding. We think in childhood home ideas, even when we act in utter contrast to our parents' ways of life. Tradition also plays a large part by keeping alive in our home experience much that has lost its vitality but continues as a mere sop to social habit, whose uselessness escapes scrutiny because its existence is interpreted as evidence of its serving social need. In this way home traditions altogether at variance with the social demands and the actual function of the individual family keep on, just like a commercialized Christmas-giving practice that has evaporated all its Christian good will.

We say the home is in transition. So it is. It is moving away from what it was toward something that it is to be. The figure conveys to some the idea that the family is something long well settled that is now on the march to a new place of comfortable resting; in other words, a family largely static has been of late awakened and will soon reach a goal of good adjustment. Although it is true that the family moves by fits and starts from the necessity of meeting occasional social crises, it is not an institution usually at an equilibrium, rarely forced into change by unusual circumstances. It is always on the move in proportion to the vigor of life that within and without clamors for adjustments in harmony with the existing social situation. It is now moving to something the future alone can fully reveal, but unless science falters, thinking grows weary and placid, and civilization enters an old age of mere reminiscence, the future will find the home, as the present finds it, with its inward stress and its outward strain, still going forward towards its illusive goal.

The home problem, therefore, is not one that we can finally solve. The perpetual friction between what is and what is to be will always be felt in the family, expressing the incompatibility of characteristic representatives of different generations and of contemporary types that are products of antagonistic social influences, and inherently unlike in personality makeup. Our present compromises, our rationalization, our archaic practices and traditions and anarchy of restless protests are what must be expected when civilization has the vitality to carry its load of human welfare forward.

The family that now is, in spite of its high degree of restlessness and its unmistakably transient character, has substance worthy of analysis as well as a prophecy of what is close at hand. It is futile to look ahead unless we can detect the direction of the present swift current of change. This is our present task. One social change that influences the home in both its marriage and parenthood elements is the passing of man's dominance. The family has been a masculine affair. Science is rather generally agreed that this has been a characteristic of the family as far back as we can unravel by deduction past experience.

The home has reflected the desires of the male. Not in every home, not everywhere in the same degree, has masculine dominance existed. It has been, however, a clearly recognized home condition, based upon social mores of the firmness of granite. And now the basic family principle has cracked. The cause is not hard to find. Education destroys submission and subservience; it limits exploitation and creates a hunger for equality of satisfaction. Woman has finally forced herself into educational opportunity. Her entrance, compared with the length of time it usually takes social habits to change, has come literally with a rush almost unparalleled in social history. She has taken the kingdom of knowledge with violence. No barrier or limitation will she now accept in her quest for experience, unless convinced by the hard logic of her own trial.

Whether man is to be hampered by the new woman, as woman has been by the man of the past, or whether there can be for most men and women not only a satisfactory division of labor, but also of self-expression, time, which lifts the curtain upon the social stage, alone can reveal.

We cannot even know what woman's dominance would mean. Since woman has been
most submissive to man in her psychic attitudes, and has formed her personality to man's
liking as the woman of China used to mutilate
her feet for the purpose of pleasing man, even
the so-called new woman, the first product of
recent changes, gives little clue to the character of the future woman, from birth free
from social traditions colored by man's dominance. Experience may prove that the woman
that has accepted man's dominance has been
the fundamentally woman-like type and the
future home, after a period of violent social
collision, will settle down to something much
like what has been.

On the contrary—as seems most probable
—home life may never again be so masculine
in its center of authority, so much a man-made
institution.

Man's power in the past has been in large
measure economic. Woman's industrial independence influences not only marriage,
but even more the family that follows
after marriage. The woman that has supported herself in any kind of business enters

marriage with ideals that are colored by her economic experiences. If she has tasted and enjoyed gregarious and competitive life in any form of commerce or industry, she sees marriage, and especially its housekeeping side, from a different angle than when she was an economic dependent.

Social thought as a means of control reflects the changes that are taking place; and the most popular, everyday thought of press, theater, or novel discloses little that can be made use of to put the home back into its former status of masculine dominance. Social pressure, even in its attitude toward an increasing divorce-rate, is moving rapidly away from any attempt at effective protest, and such pressure as remains is less and less responded to by the educated woman. The woman of culture is in the forefront in a class by herself, but the women that follow will surely move on in the same general direction. Ideas as well as styles are transmitted by prestige.

To-day men and women are sharply at odds. Especially does this seem to be true of the educated young man and woman. The former sees in his possible wife the general likeness of his mother. Although he expects a home different from that of his boyhood, he still pictures his wife in the helpmate character of his mother—a new home, but an old-fashioned type of wife. As he has let sentiment and desire turn him backward so the woman he marries has been forced by her social experience to look forward. They marry with ideals separated by a whole generation. The result is too frequently that marriage becomes an experiment in which either toleration or conflict soon becomes its very essence.

Parenthood tends more and more to be a choice. It would be more an act of volition if science had advanced to the point of making this possible. At least the idea of voluntary parenthood is assumed with a layman's confidence, and colors the philosophy of marriage almost as much as it would if we actually had a satisfactory form of contraceptive birth control.

The quantity of parenthood also has become a choice. Women give much or little to their children according to their idea of social values. Once only the shiftless and the wealthy could farm out their parenthood functions. Now both men and women in every class can to a large and dangerous degree do so if they will. From no quarter—church, school, press—comes an effective pressure that can control the policy of individual parents.

Women, moreover, although married, are not necessarily actual or even potential child-bearers. Their biological function has been subordinated and even suppressed by their response to social opportunity.

New tasks have been placed upon the schools. The desire of parents to escape responsibility has been met by a menacing eagerness of institutions to take up what fathers and mothers are all too glad to drop. Especially has this been true of the school. And schools are bound to be more aggressive in the future. Institutional ambition is motive enough. Institutions have will-to-power just as have persons, and they rationalize their cravings until they see their desires as programmes necessary for the public good. Moreover, those who deal with family failures instead of attempting to increase home efficiency are apt to turn to the more responsive school system as a means of reform. The present suspicion of parenthood is based upon the growing evidences of the power for evil of ignorant parenthood when it deals with the growing child in traditional ways that science now knows to be distinctly harmful. This skepticism will doubtless give way in time to an understanding of the indispensable value of a child's having a quantity of parental influences, if only they are socially wholesome.

The school does its present task of social adjustment with such discouraging results that it ought to restrain its institutional hunger from taking on more. Since the policy of asking for additional power covers up the shortcomings of any institution, the school will naturally ask to have the child for a longer day and to control his experience to an extent that will encourage some homes to become mere breeding and boarding places.

And strangest of all, the school, at the very time it asks for more of the child's time, still practices a selection of instructors that results in its contented women teachers becoming a type of ascetics with weak motherhood cravings; or it forces, by institutional edict, those fully endowed with human impulses to give up all hope of a home life of their own so long as they teach. Our experience with orphan asylums has taught us that children need mothers. If parents are to escape more of parenthood responsibilities, and schools are to take so much of the child's time and energy, the schools should at least provide a place for the married woman and the mother of children who wishes to return to teaching as her home duties lessen. Children who become emotional orphans, stranded between an abridged parenthood and an impersonal school, will carry through life a socially dangerous void.

The family of man's dominance had in its program the coming of children and the training of children in the home. The new order provides a freedom that gives woman much choice whether she will be a mother, and how much of a mother she will be. If the new situation is to be a social advantage modern woman needs a keener sense of social values and social responsibility.

Another social influence that is changing home life, both marriage and parenthood, is found in the modern opportunities for material culture. This is often defined as materialism by those who desire to condemn it. Love of material advantages is not without its moral dangers, and the risk of an intense quest for things appears in home life. Nevertheless we must not forget that a compelling motive that has led to social evolution and social progress has been this same desire for increased material satisfactions.

The difficulty is not that we have too much comfort or too great abundance of material luxury. It is rather that the growing resources piled up by material science are accumulating faster than man's self-control, which should keep apace of his material achievement, and much faster than man's sense of values in the use of his new advantages. It would be easier if physical science would slow down so that social science and the moral institutions might catch up. The stimulus that forces physical science forward is too strong for us to expect any relief from a decrease in material achievement.

The primitive home was an institution in harmony with the meagerness of simple life. The recent homestead family was adapted, just as the present thoroughly rural family is, to limited leisure and a life with little material surplus.

In spite of the spread of the results of applied science and the wider distribution of luxury, with the ever lessening quantity of housekeeping and home responsibilities, to many modern women their household duties seem a greater burden, a larger obstacle to pleasure, than the more strenuous family program of two generations ago appeared to the housewife of that day.

As a result, the homestead family is to a considerable degree passing, and is being replaced by a type of home that can function in the small apartment, the flat, or even the hotel. The surburban home is a compromise. It selects the small house with restricted quarters and farms out more and more of its functions, just as does the city family. The rural family still struggles with the homestead plant, but its equipment has become a problem for the housewife, and one of the reasons for rural backwardness and social dissatisfaction. In another generation it will seem a more serious handicap to the rural woman.

Housekeeping is stripped of many of its

time-consuming duties. Even in its restricted
form it is not and cannot be made to be a
stimulating ideal for the great mass of young
women. It is tolerated rather than enjoyed
by most women who have tasted at the feast
of material achievement. This is not strange
when the husbands of these very women have
turned away from manual labor and limit their
exercise to recreation. If the housework of
to-day permits a short day, housekeeping,
nevertheless, is for the majority a toilsome
occupation, largely a type of unskilled labor.
Even when most skilfully performed, it is mis-
cellaneous and repetitious in character, and
gives less sense of achievement than the work
of the husband. As one woman has said,
' Housework seems to rot the mind.'

Commerce has come to help woman
immensely; as a consequence the housekeeping is being more and more farmed out.
There is every reason to suppose that this
tendency will continue. With the scattering
of the household tasks, other home activities
have been given up; recreation especially has
changed from a family affair to an individual
experience which gives the family group less

basis for common understanding and less need of each other. Although the efficient family still finds opportunities for group recreation, the trend is certain.

It is hopeless to suppose that the increase of leisure of the average woman will be used with profit. Even when the luxury of leisure was restricted to a small and distinguished class who realized that all eyes were upon them, human nature found the ordeal too exacting. What must we expect when the multitude who wish to use their leisure in easy-going pleasure are themselves numerous enough to establish social standards in agreement with their purposes?

For some time to come the new leisure will be a social waste. Woman will be more open to criticism than man only when her leisure comes in greater abundance. There will be positive faults more serious than mere waste, as woman obtains this most testing of all luxuries, leisure. She will become, when she fails in her social trial, discontented, restless, parasitic, shirking, and intolerant of home obligations. If, on the other hand, she has talent, a career or a part-time career in addition to that of home-making will be for her the opportunity for satisfying achievement.

The full force of the attraction of material culture does not show itself with reference to the home until we notice that it is largely responsible for a new type of marriage. Marriage in the past centered about children. It was an institution that grew out of the need of protecting the helpless child. Although it has never been the usual thing for young people to marry with the conscious motive of having children, it has been taken for granted that in due time children would come. At present, marriage often starts with the deliberate intent of husband and wife or of wife alone that there shall be no children. If children do come, it is because of the failure of the married couple to carry out their program.

Since there is usually no economic advantage in marriage, outside the rural environment, sex has to assume the task of providing a basis for the home. Sex, as an idealized, motivating attraction, impels toward marriage and provides its beginning. When it becomes an end in itself, the marriage has an abnormal degree of hazard. Sex as an impulse is notoriously unsteady; also when separated from comradeship and parenthood it is tyrannous and frequently undermines rather than establishes permanent relationship between a man and a woman.

A marriage that has for its sole program the production of immediate pleasure and the establishment of mutual convenience has no basis for normal growth. It may or may not eventually awaken to the need of children. Parenthood impulses as a rule enter consciousness only as a result of concrete, specific stimulus, either the presence of the child or the knowledge of the child's coming. With only sex and comfort as motives, and no functioning of parental love, there is little to protect restless couples from divorce.

Protests against divorce are largely negative. The separation of people who no longer have interests in common is frowned upon. Next to nothing is done, nevertheless, to lift marriage above sex—the stress of adultery as a satisfactory reason for divorce gives emphasis to the physical sex element in marriage. To avoid divorce, marriage must, in these days of psychic cravings, develop into a human

relationship that contains much more than
sex. This is difficult when a narrow sense of
pleasure, an unwillingness to accept economic
burdens or to sacrifice freedom, prevents the
coming of children. The desire for pleasure,
especially in cases where the woman has had
economic independence in industry, makes the
distribution of the family income a cause of
division and even of hostility.

All in all, materialism has given the family
its most staggering blow. The home still
recovers in countless cases because the program of no children does not work out as
was confidently expected, since science does
not yet possess the contraceptive control of
birth that is so generally supposed. Nature
leads the self-seekers through parenthood into
a larger marriage experience than mere physical advantage can accomplish. If contraceptive birth control becomes positive in its
certainty, modern marriage must face a severe
testing.

The predicament of the present family is at
bottom the result of science. The source of our
modern civilization is science, but a badly bal-
anced science. Science, the thing-maker,

flourishes. Science is too largely captive to economic profit, chained, as it were, to its workshop. Science as a way of dealing with life without bias and with the fullest resources available is something more than a mere slave substitute for economic production. It is therefore the want of science in the larger sense that hampers most the modern home. Science not only can heat homes and decrease drudgery: it also can give a strategic insight into the conditions that make for happy marriage and wholesome parenthood.

The new woman and the new man are to some extent turning to science for marriage guidance. Love is not, among the educated, as blind as once it was. It considers many things. An ever increasing body of conscientious youth ask for scientific assistance. The venereal disease risk, for example, is faced frankly, and the need of examination of both men and women before marriage is more and more taken for granted by both sexes. The more thoughtful turn to the science of eugenics with such questions as: Is our proposed marriage right? Are we fit to have children? Some are also coming to the sociologists for advice regarding engagement and marriage, believing that science can detect incompatibilities before marriage experiences reveal them.

We need more science in the home. Unless parents are to be denied the control and companionship of their children practically from birth, they must be taught, for psychiatry is showing that what the parents do in the first years of childhood has the profoundest social influence upon personality. Why let parents ignorantly spoil children and then spend social energy in attempting to reform the individual who has suffered from unwise parental treatment? It must be remembered that educated people do not necessarily make educated parents. The instruction must be specifically applied to parenthood.

Schools need to prepare for such instruction by building up a sense of the value and meaning of science. The best product of a school intellectually is the establishment in the mind of youth of an appreciation that the scientific way of dealing with any problem is the only good way. Once this is generally accomplished, we can use our present re-

sources of science for the advantage of those
who have young children to train. The super-
stitions, the cruel traditions that intelligent
parents still follow in the control of children,
are the saddest revelation in life of the meager
sense the average person has of the practical
value of psychological and sociological science.
Mental hygiene has assumed the task of bringing science into human behavior, but it ought
not to have the work to do all alone. Sociology is committed to the task of understanding people in their social behavior, and out
of human experience it must gather whatever
it is to offer a socially retarded civilization.
Mental hygiene is influencing men and women
in their social relationships in a practical way
that makes an observer question whether it is
not the nearest approach to an applied sociology that actually functions.

That the home is in trouble no one doubts.
It has by no means passed its crisis. In spite
of its lessening importance, it is still the strategic source of social control, the institution
that chiefly forms personality. Its condition
challenges the science that is most concerned
with problems of social welfare. More diffi-

cult to study than other institutions, because of its privacy and reticence, its problem is the one that thoughtful people wish better understood. The sociologist, in dealing with it, has the same obligation that the psychiatrist found in the prevalence of mental disease. There is the same imperative necessity of bringing science in popular form to a great multitude who in their everyday life need the help it has to give. If home life is to be conserved, it must have the advantages of applied science.

$$\frac{\begin{array}{r} 37 \\ 24 \end{array}}{6}$$

CHAPTER III

WHAT CAN THE FAMILY DO?

THE community is stripping the family of its old-time functions so persistently that many people are shaking their heads and wondering where this will end. How much longer can the family withstand the concerted attack of all the different social organizations that are sure they can do its work far better than the family itself? The school man, the social worker and the minister are inclined to think their success in meeting the wants of children justifies their taking over still more of the former duties of parents. Some have lost their courage regarding the family's ability to get on satisfactorily, no matter how much help they give it.

But the family itself looks at the matter quite differently. It is glad to turn over to specialists the varied departments of its responsibility, since it knows that no one couple can hope to vie with experts who concentrate their attention solely on educating the child or maintaining and improving his health or providing for him socialized recreation or furnishing him with moral leadership. The family has risen from the position of maid-of-all-work to that of administrator: instead of attending to all the details of the child's care it supervises the work of the underlings to whom it has farmed out its interests. Standing in the center of the child's life, observing his special activities, it can weigh the value of the eager efforts of its department heads and keep them from developing their own skill at the expense of the child's all-round welfare.

It is easy for the institutional mind to see the child only as grist for its own mill. The school official thinks first of pouring into the child information, of enabling him to pass a good oral or written examination, and last or not at all of the effect on the child's physical well-being of the long hours he spends cooped up indoors with his fundamental muscles lax and his breathing shallow or of the effect on his social development of his sitting for hours every day with twenty or thirty children of his own age, engaged on similar problems, but unable to converse freely with the others about his work or his thoughts. The health worker is too engrossed in watching the scales go up or measuring the chest expansion to take much thought about the inferiority complexes that are likely to beset the children whom he puts down as anæmic, undersized, or having a weak heart. The social worker is too busy helping to straighten out the difficulties of the sick, poor, abused or ' bad ' child to pay attention to the troubles or needs of the ordinary child with whom he has contact. The religious leader sees the child only in special situations and can have little knowledge of his everyday personal behavior.

It is in the home that the child shows up as an individual rather than an item in the day's work of some organization or a speck in the mass of children being put through any definite institutional procedure. Here he throws off restraint and allows his own preferences to determine his conduct, thus revealing to his parents more of his natural bent than he shows to outsiders. From the parent the child does not hide his chafing under some of the coercion put upon him when he is away from home nor does he, when at home, have to check the expression of his delight in those activities that please him; hence the parent better than other workers with children can see what guidance and encouragement a particular child needs, and get him to appreciate the value of those experiences whose meaning he has failed to catch.

No matter how much the family gives over to organized interests the care of its children, it will continue to discharge its most important functions since they cannot well be taken care of by any institution but itself. As the school, the playground, clubs, municipal movements, and the church furnish the child more and more of his opportunities for action, the family must try to interpret to him his daily experiences away from the roof-tree. When the child comes home from institutions that cater to him, with his story of the day's happenings, the wise parent will get the child to talk with him about his experiences and help him to understand what his games and clubs and other organizations do for him and for society. The family will be the great interpreter rather than the minister of resources. The more efficient society becomes in providing equipment and organizations to do the work that used to be done by the family, the less the family has to do for the child, but the little that is left in its own hands is indispensable because the other organizations are too busy to have any time to do much interpreting, and if they did attempt it their specialization would make each of them overemphasize its own share.

The family also keeps the power of directing the child to a great extent. If he goes to one school rather than to another, if he takes up one kind of club work instead of another, he gets different results. The parent can counsel him about his choice of institutions and activities, giving him an inkling of what he is likely to get from it before he ties himself up with an organization. Those parents who are not wasting their time and strength in trying to compete with outside resources are best able to direct their children in making decisions as to which out-of-the-home interests they will get most out of in the long run.

The family must stimulate the child to make full use of his opportunities. Families that are frantically trying to duplicate the work of outside agencies in serving their children, worried lest they are losing their power, are neglecting their greater privilege of stimulating the children. A prominent educator who is famous for the quickness with which he has prepared children for college says that his scheme was primarily stimulating the child, particularly by using mealtime for discussion of the values and arresting singularities of the subjects the children were about to study.

A parent can arouse a child's interest with very little effort by talking with him or carrying on discussions in his presence. Many a person could testify as Dr. Richard C. Cabot does:

' As I remember my own childhood, I think nothing helped me so much as what I saw call out the unfeigned and spontaneous enthusiasm of my elders. When they glowed, crackled, or exploded with delight over a book read aloud, over someone's bravery, over a fern, after a piece of music, over a promise maintained in difficulties, and were not aware of my presence or trying to set me an example, then I inwardly and almost unconsciously marked and was marked by the action of

reality.   I looked, as every child does, through
the eyes and through the actions of my elders
(parents, brothers, friends), and was moulded
not directly by them but by something greater
than they, something to which they unmistakably looked up.'

It is not necessary that the parent have a
deep understanding of every advanced subject
his child is going to take up, but he does need
to show the small child the power of study
to give him the ability and understanding he
craves. The child that hurls puzzling questions at his mother and father has to be told
sometimes, ' That is all I know about it; when
you study physics you will find out just how
it happens.'   Then the youngster grows up
with the idea that physics is a subject full of
value for him, so that he will bring to its
study an eager curiosity that will melt away
its difficulties and enable him to make his
knowledge of this science a very real part of
his equipment: to a child prepared in this
everyday, incidental way for his entry upon
the field of science, physics can never be
merely a hard, dry subject to be passed off in
order to get into college or out of high school.

As the child goes out into the community he gets the results of his home stimulation. He can be made to use the library, to go in for sports or other physical activities, to look out for his own health and that of his mates, to do whatever his parents have interested him in doing. No parent can interest all his children in the same things, but he can offer them enough different avenues of possible interest so that each of them will be accelerated in the lines of action he follows and will make a wider choice of work and play than if left to himself. The child who receives little concrete stimulation at home often takes one subject rather than another or joins one club rather than another just because that is what his next-door neighbor is doing. It is sometimes pitiful to see this type of college student planning his course of study, taking one subject because his roommate takes it, another because it does not come too early in the morning, a third because it has the ' rep ' of being easy, and a fourth because it fits into his schedule so that he will have free time in the pleasantest part of the day or because it is a two-hour course—that boon to the drifting student—and will enable him to avoid loading up with one more hour's work than he is required to take.

Stimulation must come chiefly from the home. Teachers and other workers with children are too busy meeting definite goals of achievement with the mass of young people entrusted to them to be able to spend much time in awakening in their charges the attitude of mind that makes their powers function. Nobody who sees young people only in large groups can understand them as individuals well enough to give them much of the stimulation they need. There will never be a time when any of our institutions can depend on their own stimulating power, yet their work with children who receive little stimulation drags and accomplishes little. The children who are stimulated by their parents are a joy to those who work with them outside the home.

Another thing the parent must always do for the child, no matter how much outside agencies are doing for him, is to give to the child fellowship. A child needs fellowship with his parents far more than we realize. We know that children cared for in the finest orphan asylums have a more slender chance of living to maturity than the children in the very poorest homes in the congested quarters of cities. It is the lack of individual love and fellowship that cuts down the orphan's life-expectation, say the workers in charge. Within separate homes the amount of fellowship the children get is an important factor in determining how happily they will go through life. Few children who have fellowshipped with their parents get into really serious behavior difficulties.

Teachers, ministers and other social workers cannot fellowship with their children, partly because they have too many and partly because such fellowship is less natural than in the case of the parent. There are likely to be misinterpretations of fellowship if it is very close between a child and an older person not related to him. We are always a little critical when we see a teacher or social worker much with a child, and we have some reason for our feeling, since every little while we find that this fellowship is not wholesome. Ordinarily the only person who has the right attitude and a free opportunity for fellowship is the parent.   Nobody ever criticizes the parent for being much with his child.   Indeed, unwholesomeness does sometimes occur here, but that is only when the parent interprets fellowship as monopoly, and tries to make the child perpetually dependent on him.   There is no danger of the fellowship of parent and child being excessive in quantity; it is its quality that is liable to be at fault, but that is when real fellowship does not exist and its name is used as a cloak for the dependence of either parent or child on the other.   True fellowship between parent and child is the last stronghold of the family which can never be evacuated.

As long as the family keeps in its grasp all these important functions, it need not insist on doing the medical work, cooking the food, making the clothes, or having a great part of the child's life so far as the time element is concerned.   Perhaps the community, which is so efficiently organized, should be given more of this type of work to do for the child. If the mother is too busy to bring up her little child satisfactorily, we ought not to complain when a nursery school takes the child over at two or three, provided the family does its own part in fellowshipping, stimulating, directing, and interpreting. The family that is relieved of its burdensome routine of detail is able to concentrate on its four great functions and therefore can better discharge its responsibilities.

Sentiment is strong against the departure of the very young child from the home to the school, but at whatever age the child first flutters out of the home-nest, the mother always mourns his going. Putting aside sentiment we must think of this as of other problems from the child's point of view. Must the parent teach the child to talk? Whatever advantage we may see in that, we know that most cases of lisping, slovenly speech and bad enunciation are directly traceable to the imitation of the parent or somebody else within the home by the child of two or three. Would it not be far better if we were taught to speak by persons who are specialists in the use of the voice?

There is no danger of the family's crumbling just because it gives up some of its old-time functions, if it keeps its directing power.

We no longer feel that the parent should make all the clothes of the child; we are coming to see that the parent need not cook all the child's food or teach him all his behavior. In fact, the nursery school often teaches the child in a few weeks habits the parents have not been able to teach him in years. The child who leaves his toys lying all over the house and cannot be taught to put them away goes to the nursery school and is urged by the other children to help them tidy up; he soon does eagerly what he sees the rest doing, and when he goes home announces, ' I know how to pick up my toys and put them in the play-cupboard,' then proudly demonstrates his new ability. It is easier to get a child to conform to the standards of the nursery school than of the home because he feels so keenly the social pressure exerted by children of his own age.

The family that fails to do well by its children is usually the family that fails to recognize what it ought to be doing. It is still trying to do the things it once had to do because there was nobody else to do them. This family is like the very bad executive who tries to do everything himself.   Once I went by the office of an administrator in a large institution and found one of the officials sweeping the sidewalk.   Assuming that he was not out for exercise, but was doing this because he felt the janitor had not done it properly, my guide's criticism was well made: ' There is a man who wants everything done right; if others don't do as he thinks they should, he does their work for them.   He is always behind in his own work because he won't trust those under him to carry out their own functions.'   That is very bad administration. The good administrator picks his men and removes them if they do not do their work. The family that thinks it must give the child most of his education and moral training and his amusements, fearful lest the outside world will capture the functions of the family, is like the executive who does not know what belongs to him and does things that can be done better by subordinates who are skillful in their particular line.

The family has not lost its strategic position, for, though it has given up some things and may give up more, it has done this in

order that it may have more time and capacity
to function along its most important lines with
success. If a mother gets tired because she
does every little thing a child needs done, unwilling to have outside help of any sort, she
is unfit to give the child what a mother can
give him best. She is too tired to interpret
life, too busy to find out how to help him
direct his life. Perhaps she does not pay
much attention to what happens outside the
home; she just works. As a husband said to
me the other day, ' My wife is not well and it
is partly because she is so busy working for
the children, she has no time for anything
else.' This woman is doing the less important
work; she does not have time to function as
the mother must function in the modern
world.

It is impossible for us to live to-day the
simple life that once was common. The family,
like other institutions, must adjust itself to
these changed circumstances; it gives up some
of its duties that it may have more opportunity. The mother that is not overworked in
the trivialities of life is going to be the best
sort of mother. The father who has to work

hard to earn a living sometimes envies wealthy parents' advantage in having more time to give their children. The father and mother who will let the community do all it can for their children are free to place whatever time they can spare where it will do the most good — in stimulating and directing their children, interpreting life to them and fellowshipping with them.

I know a woman who fed and dressed her child with great skill and managed her house remarkably well. This mother took care of the child's daily life, but she had no time to study the problems of life and she gave the child no fellowship. The daughter was so left by herself that in spite of her careful training she became an unmarried mother; even in this situation she would not allow her mother to try to help her, but said, ' My mother has never helped me. She can do nothing for me now.' The mother had been a servant, a dress-maker, a cook. Had she been a true mother, the problem that finally resulted would never have occurred.

The family function henceforth will not be cooking, sewing, teaching, but providing a source whence the child will draw his standards. The community organizations must act in accordance with the desires of the family, for the chief object of these organizations and their enterprises is the well-being of the family. None of the community activities could function in a thoroughly satisfactory way if the family did not leaven the community with its own distinctive attitude. The supreme testing of the efficiency of the community is in the hands of the family.

If, without a noticeable lowering in the quality of work done, it is to continue parceling out its work to outside agencies, the family must pass in review its various subordinates and check up on the results they are obtaining. The family will scrutinize most closely the schools, since to them it has delegated the largest share in its responsibility. The first criticism to be passed is that the tendency of the schools to be mechanical disqualifies them as substitutes for the home, especially in the early period of the child's life. Of course there are families that are mechanical, where everybody gets up at the same time, eats and works by the clock, and plays only at stated intervals, but that is not the average American family; it is too artificial, does not adjust itself to variations.

Yet the school, because of its large responsibilities, its great number of children, and its insistence on the reaching of definite goals of accomplishment, is run on the same lines that are characteristic of the factories where everybody works with his mind on the clock. A considerable number of prominent school officials believe that is the sort of training children need, and pride themselves on the mechanical efficiency of their schools. The family says to the schools: ' If you are to take our children more, for our advantage and for theirs, you must not treat them as if they were raw material to be manipulated according to your process, but you must think of them as human beings who above everything else need an enormous amount of freedom that in the past you have not been able to give them. Before you take over our children more than at present, won't you be quite sure to stop putting so much stress on your standardized results, for such a practice is not at all like home life and you are now substitutes for the home?

In our really good homes we don't expect all our children to play and work alike, enjoy the same things, dress the same, and think about the same things at the same time. We expect them to be different and so we demand of you that you let them be different.'

That seems a very simple thing to ask, but the schools cannot at present comply with the family's demand; they are too mechanical and too standardized. Unless they change their ways they will make the children into less-balanced individuals than when they did not get the children so young, but waited until the home had given them a good start. Children who are very rapidly standardized become either too docile or too rebellious. The attention and activity of the school is largely concerned with making its own processes operate smoothly rather than with criticizing them and adjusting them to life. Each department seems to exist for itself with little regard for the welfare of the child whom it supposedly serves.

If you find fault with any part of this departmental egotism you step at once into a squirrel cage, and go round and round trying to get some one to admit that he has the power to change the situation, though every one agrees with you that it should be changed. Suppose you criticize the primary-school teacher of English; her answer is, 'I don't approve of much that I am doing, but I have to do it to get my children ready to meet the demands of the grammar-school teachers.'

You leave the lower-grade teacher and go to the grammar-school teacher, saying, 'The primary English teacher wants to give the child what he needs, but she can't because she has to get him ready for your requirements. Why don't you let her teach as she wants to? You know it would be better for the child.' The grammar-school teacher agrees, but tells you that she has all she can do to get her children ready for high school and it is out of the question for her to loosen the thumb-screws she has put on the primary teacher, or to do her own teaching in any different way than she is doing it, though she knows she is not doing wisely from the child's viewpoint, and he is really the one that should be considered, not the high-school teacher.

'I, too, am helpless,' says the high-school

teacher; ' I am just a cog in a machine; I have to insist that the grammar-school teacher do things I know to be worthless or even harmful, so far as getting the child to use good English and to love the best in literature is concerned. I am just as badly off, myself, for the college lays its heavy hand on my work and I flurry around trying to do what I must if I am to hold my job, all the time seeing my children turned from the very goal we all pretend to think we are driving them toward.   It is no use. I cannot serve the child and the System, and I have chosen to serve the System, for I must live; but it is hard. You see I happen to love literature, and I would like to help my pupils to enjoy, appreciate, and perhaps pro- duce some. Instead, I keep my hundred and fifty boys and girls for a year on six books, learning facts that will come in handy in ex- amination time. How they loathe those books when we are through with them, and how care- fully they afterward steer clear of any books suggestive of them! Why don't the colleges wake up and hear the birds sing? If they would just let us do for our children what needs to be done, without reference to yardstick requirements, I'm thinking the college English teachers would be greatly surprised to see how much better prepared our students would be — not for taking college entrance examinations, but for doing work of college grade.'

The college teacher of English is just as perturbed and helpless as the rest. He says: ' People expect a college graduate to be conversant with certain trends and achievements in the world of letters; he must be a cultured type. That gives us a vast amount to accomplish; even with all the help we can get from the elementary and secondary schools, we are hard put to it to come anywhere near the goal that is set for us by the public. It is possible that different methods in the grades and high school would bring better results, but I dare not encourage any experimenting; it might mean years of failure that would lower the enrollment of my college and permanently injure its reputation. If anything is done, it must be by the concerted action of all the colleges, or by the clubbing together of all the high schools in a refusal to go on complying with our demands. It is strange how all-power-

ful the high schools think us. We are not so
strong as they. We serve only a small percentage of their students, and that percentage
is selected largely on the basis of their fathers'
pocketbooks, not on the basis of scholarship
alone. If the high schools would just stand
by each other in their determination to do for
their students what they think ought to be
done, what could we do? We should have to
accept the students the high schools chose to
send us, or go out of business. The first twelve
years of the public school system were not
created for the sake of the colleges, and, being far bigger and stronger than we, they can
preserve their individuality if they will. The
blame is not ours, but the public's. The tax-
payers, who support the schools, must insist
that the interests of the great majority who
have no thought of going to college be given
first place; and incidentally the college-going
youth will benefit as much as the others by
a programme that takes account primarily of
the needs of the growing child himself, in
every year of his schooling. Talk to the parents; this problem is surely up to them.'

The schools are running a closed system,

with every department trying to fit in with the other departments and, in its concentration on departmental efficiency, ignoring its opportunity to study and help the child. It is as if a housekeeper were so intent on keeping the habitation immaculate and improving her decorative scheme that she neglected to cook the dinner and refused to let any member of the family set foot in the dining-room, living-room, or drawing-room lest he ' muss it up.' The schools, like every other organization, are beset with the danger that they become so involved in their own processes as to lose sight of their reason for existence and substitute for their real objectives the accidental habits into which they have fallen.

The home will lay concrete obligations on the school, especially when it sends its three-year-olds commonly, as it soon will. ' The school must give the child more outdoor freedom. At present the high school is making a movement toward a longer day; it should be driving in just the opposite direction. A shorter day in the schoolroom with more time for free activity out of doors is what the children need. The things the children do in the school period seem very important until one looks at them to see what value they have as a function of life, when they dwindle almost into nothingness. By keeping the children indoors and putting them to work mentally so much of the time, you are denying them their full heritage of physical health and race vitality. The body was not made for sitting quietly in the house from nine to four, and it cannot change to adjust itself to the new mode of life without serious loss of power. During the thousands of years man has been on the earth he has spent his time very differently. The body will not adapt itself to its new circumstances, save at the expense of its vigor. This means that the child's daily schedule must be changed if he is not to be seriously hampered in his career by a weak body.'

The home also says to the school: ' Our children used to be outdoors a good deal. Don't keep them in the house so much, and don't meddle with them. When we were taking care of them, we let them alone; we did not run out every fifteen minutes and tell them to do something else. You are constantly deciding for them what they must do and making them all follow. If anybody lags behind, you think he is feeble-minded. Treat your children like human beings, not like mechanisms that will march around at the stroke of the bell. Let them have freedom and opportunity to discover themselves. That takes skill on your part, for it is difficult for any instructor to keep himself sufficiently in the background, but if you do manage it you will be rewarded by finding interesting variations in your children. At present you have not attained to the point of view that allows you to enjoy individual variations in your charges, but that is partly because your strict adherence to rules and regulations plays havoc with your sense of humor. Anything out of the ordinary in your orthodox upper grades worries you exceedingly. If you have a child that does not spell, you almost want to cut him off. By great exertion you may succeed in making him a good speller, but only after such expenditure of effort that you have prevented his doing other more important things. This does not matter so much with the older child of the upper grades as it does when it happens to the younger one who feels more deeply your influence. With the younger child you must do as the parents did when he was entirely under their care, let Nature decide how he is to act, expressing itself differently in each child, so that every grown-up person will be quite unlike his neighbors.

'Have you the willingness to allow this diversity of personal endowment to flower unhindered, or are you too mechanical to meet this situation? If you cannot do it, the day when the little child leaves home for a nursery school will be accursed, for human nature cannot stand unyielding coercion and uniformity, especially in the first years, without losing all the spontaneity that carries a person to success. You have only one alternative: either you will allow freedom and encourage variation, or you will get a dull-minded flock of people that can be easily led, while those that cannot bear to run hither and yon at your beck will be rebels who will vex society because they will be always preying on it at one point or another. This giving of freedom to the child cannot be on paper only, as so much in our schools is. It must be actual. Eventually you may get the child soon after birth, but you must show more willingness to let his variations appear or your power will be against his best possibilities and against the welfare of society.'

The home spirit, when it faces the greater passing of the child into the hands of the school, is very determined that the school must adjust itself and become somewhat as the home used to be if it is to do well by the child. If the school will do this, the child will be even better off than he could be if he were kept at home longer, for he needs the companionship of youngsters of his own age.

Just as the school will try to take over more and more of the supervision of the child's intellectual life, so the church will also attempt to gain more of his moral and religious life. The way this may be done is by making the church a part of the school process so that the child going to school will automatically be at church part of the time, and the church school will prevail. The defense for this programme is that the church no longer reaches the lives of the great mass of young people, and their religious training must not be neglected; a well-ordered school programme is what they need rather than the haphazard teaching they are picking up from each other. It may be true that the child must go to school to learn about morals and religion as far as those things can be definitely taught. If that happens, the home will have a word to say to the church school: ' You must do for the child what we used to do in the home. We gave him a child's home religion which is very different from what you have for him. In your programme we find a great deal of adult and theological interest; even philosophical material creeps into your teaching, and we know that is not what we taught our children at the fireside at bedtime. Our religion was a very simple one, as religion must be when it is vigorous. From its very nature it is weakened by complication. What we tried to teach had to do with the behavior of the child in his everyday life. If we told Bible stories they were stories that applied directly to the child's daily doings; we also told fairy stories with the same purpose. Stories with a moral that the child could see and make use of were what we gave him. Everything was very simple and natural. We were parents and the kind of religion we wanted in our children was adapted to their needs and our own and had to do with life as it came to the child day by day. Will you try to do as we have done, in teaching our children? If you will, you can do better than we, for we no longer have the time nor the foundation of common interests on which to build our practical religious teaching; but we are afraid when you get our children you will begin to inoculate them with theological doctrines characteristic of adults, and we know that will spoil them, make them irreligious, make them unwholesome, because it will attempt to make them precocious, and precocity is the bane of healthy childhood. We want you to stress kindly, but sensible behavior. Your teaching must be so simple that no one in the world can tell by listening to you whether you are Catholic, Protestant, Jew, or Mohammedan. In the old days you could not tell with reference to the mother's teaching. Sometimes she thought she had sectarian differences in her teaching, but what she gave her children was generally a universal attitude rather than a denominational one.

' You must do something else that is very

hard for you to do, and that you have never
been able to do with adults. You must make
your pupils grow beyond your teaching. When
you have approached adults you have almost
always been well satisfied if you could get
them to accept your present teaching. You
have had an air of finality. The result is that
your teaching is no more progressive than
you are yourself. Every little while difficulty
arises because some of your people, particularly of the younger generation, are more progressive than you are. You must remember
that these children will live longer than you do
and they must be ready for the future. Otherwise disaster will come out of this church
teaching of all the little children, for you will
close and stagnate their minds more than if
you left them alone. It is a hard task for you
to adapt yourself to teaching little children.
If you cannot do it, you had better have us
start again trying to do it ourselves.'

The home must judge industry also from
the family point of view. Various types of industry are keenly competing against the
family, although in certain lines the shorten-
ing of the hours of labor has somewhat modi-

fied this competition. Aside from the time spent away from home, most parents give so much of their vitality to industry that they cannot pay their children nearly as much attention as they used to when parents and children worked together on the farm. The father goes in the morning to the office, factory, or store and comes back at night with every ounce of energy, that he feels like spending, gone. What is left for the child? On holidays the father does not dare give much time to the child, lest he get too tired for the next day's competition. Industry has greatly impeded the parent's discharge of his obligations in the home. To industry the family says: ' Do you realize that we do not judge industry by its efficiency in wealth-producing activities? We judge it by what it does to people, not by what it makes for them. As a socially functioning industry the test you must pass is whether you produce better men and women than used to be produced under other industrial conditions; if you are willing to try to meet that demand, you must recognize in your business policy that you are dealing with fathers and perhaps with mothers and you must provide for the conservation of that side of life, even though it check your competition and still further decrease the hours of labor.'

One man reports that the chief of staff in the school where he works exhorts his teachers to ' Put all the strength of which you are capable into your service for this institution. When you go home at night you are not through; you must study and keep up with your work in mind every minute that you can, regardless of whether you have any time for your families.' If a social agency can say that, it is easier to realize how indifferent most men in industry are, and how little they think of the effect of their conditions on family life. Yet the family eventually will have to pass judgment on industry and give the deciding verdict as to whether a definite business is socially justified or is a menace; this verdict will be made, not on the basis of the industry's wealth-producing efficiency, but of its effect on men and women.   That is the real test which in the end must always be met in any civilization.   Like the church and the school, industry will have to accept a family attitude as its basic concept.

A friend tells me that in a certain Massachusetts industry he has for many years watched men go to work. Most of the new men have been immigrants, strong and vigorous rural people from Central Europe, who enter the mill with vitality, perhaps with ambition. As a rule they cannot stand that labor more than seven years; then they break down, become tuberculous or otherwise diseased, or drift into easier work, broken in body. In the short span of seven years they are finished as far as working in that type of factory is concerned, many get lighter work, some go back to Europe, some finally go to the almshouse. Can anybody honestly justify that sort of thing? Has any industry the right to ask individuals to sacrifice their family and future for six or seven years of labor just because ' it pays '—somebody gets a profit out of it? The home will say to industry, ' Unless you can find some way to conserve the men who work for you, we shall have to legislate about the matter or put you out of business.'

Public taxation has its influence upon the family. The middle-class home is especially sensitive to an increasing tax burden and the mounting costs of government, especially state and municipal, encourage the smaller family. Our income tax systems, especially in the States, and our tariff rates are written with little regard to their possible effect upon family life. Tax laws are considered too narrowly as mere ways of drawing funds into the public purse, or their immediate effect upon business is given serious attention with no thought of their more remote but consequential influence upon marriage and births.

If we were as conscious of our middle-class birth-rate problem as are France, Germany, and even England, we should insist that the family be given greater consideration in the making of taxation programmes. Immigration has largely concealed our birth-rate problem. Now that the inflow of immigrants with their large families is ceasing as a result of our recent restrictive legislation, we shall be forced to recognize the native birth-rate tendency. The time when we, like France, shall be experimenting with a system of family allowances may not be so distant as we think.

The problem of employment vitally affects

the family in obvious ways. As an indispensable unit of society, the family protests against the fact that so many men are given temporary employment and at any moment sent out of the factory with nothing to do just because it does not pay for the industry to go on. In time it may be that industry will be forced to stand such losses itself and support the man whom it throws out of work, as to a large extent the English cotton mills did at the time of the cotton famine during our Civil War. Business must not take in human material, rush it at its highest speed, and then throw it out the moment work slackens. Under those circumstances wholesome life cannot be maintained. How can any business man be proud of his industry if he carries it on in that easy way? All he has to do is to keep his mill going while he is making profits, shut it when he has none. Industry must assume its just share of responsibility for wholesome family life. It must support its workers through slack periods instead of simply freeing itself of loss by stepping out from under its obligations. If this sounds far off and impossible, we may wonder if we can put an end to passions and strikes until this becomes the programme of industry.

The weapon by means of which the family can enforce its wishes on the school, the church, government, and industry is that intangible but all-powerful thing, public opinion. Not that the family has a monopoly of the use of public opinion. In fact, here as elsewhere, the earlier responsibility of the home has been greatly divided with other agencies. It is, therefore, all the more necessary that the home use what strength it has in controlling public opinion for the furtherance of its own welfare, lest competing wielders of public opinion carelessly set at naught all the attempts of the family to control its own destiny.

It is hard to tell where public opinion lodges, outside its breeding-place in the family, for it is a queer thing which, like the air, we feel, seldom stopping to think whence it comes. In so far as we can locate public opinion, we should probably say it is in the newspaper, but the newspaper is as sensitive as any other public institution to public opinion, and its editors are constantly reshaping their course according to the way the public feels about the things they publish. The newspaper reflects public opinion, intensifies it, and to some extent moulds it, but is itself bound by the public opinion of its constituents. Public opinion is in the thinking of most of us, in the feeling of all of us. We are influenced by it, and we influence it. At bottom public opinion is the determining factor in the conduct of almost any institution or person.

When the family talks to the editor, the publisher, it says: ' So far as anybody has the initiative of social control through the making of public opinion, you have it. You can hang people, let people free, elect and defeat presidents, make and change laws; you have tremendous power. We want to tell you what, as parents, we think you should do. We recognize that we shall have to let our children go out into the free play of public opinion earlier than they once did. They will dress and think and do as others do because they will receive outside influence when they are so young as to be very impressionable. Once we kept them with us and gave them public opinion in a sense until they were in their teens. Now they will have to pick it up from you. What will you give them? If you are going to take them over, we ask of you that you be friendly to the family. That is not much to ask since you are supported by people who have family interest.'

Perhaps the editor or publisher will say, 'That is too abstract. What do you mean?' 'You are inconsistent. In to-day's paper we can show you that in certain columns you are friendly and in other places—your advertisements and tricky editorials, the ones you are not proud of—you are against family life. We say it is not enough to do something on one page for family welfare if on another page a more fundamental influence is thrown against it. Are you, for instance, on the side of prohibition? No, you are not. Yet where is the family, considered as a unit with every child allowed a full voice, that would vote against prohibition? Does anybody think that on a family basis you could ever vote back the saloon? Not at all. It would be doubtful if it could be maintained in England and Scotland if the children voted too on a family basis. You know where the family's interest is on this question. But you are not thinking of the family when you give a third of your front page, with scareheads and photographs, to the romantic story of rum-runners who defy death for big stakes on the high seas. We could show you every day in almost every paper suggestions for and suggestions against family life; and we tell you, Mr. Editor, the paper the family wants is one that from beginning to end standardizes itself in harmony with family interests. We not only want all the news that is fit to read; we want all the suggestions that are good for family life.'

How this policy would change some of the material put out by the press! Newspaper men who use some very good stuff and some very poor stuff assert that they correct the harm their bad material does by publishing other material that is of constructive value, but that cannot be done, for the same person does not read both kinds of material, or chancing to read them is not equally impressed by both. Unwholesomeness cannot be counteracted by a dose of wholesomeness; all must be wholesome. It is not just the yellow press that is at fault here; sometimes the aristocratic paper is the worst offender against family welfare.

As the family gives more of the child's life to the outside world, the business of the family is not to duplicate the service of other organizations, but to supplement and unify their work by fellowshipping with the child, stimulating and directing him and interpreting life for him. The family must be responsible for the policies of the agencies that help it, and in each case the test will have to be: Do these processes square with the interests of the family? If not, then they are perverted, unwholesome, even though in their own field they seem all right. Industry, for instance, judged by its own standards, may seem very prosperous, but if its prosperity is at the cost of the family's welfare, then it is all wrong. There is nothing in the world stronger or more wholesome or more thoroughly safe than family life, and it is the place of the family to be the umpire rather than the victim of these other powerful organizations that do not have its interests at heart.

CHAPTER IV

THE HOME: A HUMAN NEED

In these days when there is an ever-growing pessimism regarding both marriage and parenthood, it is easy to forget that the family originated to fulfill a human need. The family is not something alien to human desire, forced upon people by outside pressure; it is an institution which has issued from the experience of mankind as a means of satisfying some of the profoundest cravings of our nature. The widespread distrust of the home, one of the significant social facts of our period, particularly as it expresses itself in our literature, is the product of several influences. It results from our better understanding of the ways in which family life hurts people, the contribution of recent science, especially psychoanalytic investigation of human problems; a general rise in family standards, notably material comforts, with a corresponding pushing forward of ideals of home life; less tolerance on the part of those who experience unhappy family conditions; a lessening of social pressure against family separation; and, probably most important of all, social restlessness due to the fact that we are not yet well adjusted to the new ways of living thrust upon us by modern inventions which make many demand too much of the home while at the same time reluctant to sacrifice superficial personal pleasures for its welfare.

The plight of the modern family which cannot build up a satisfying home life comes about not so much because the family type of human association fails to meet present-day human needs as because of a misconception as to what the family can and should do for its members. The family fails because its members are not able to take from their association together the satisfactions normal home life has to offer.

Doubtless the family was at first a biological necessity. Whatever it may be in the future as a result of the new scientific discoveries of which some now dream, it is still a biological necessity. Even the physical rearing of the child, we have found from actual experience, can be done best by some sort of home life; the institution, however scientifically conducted, does not do so well as the home. The human family soon added to its biological purpose a social function which made it what it still is, the most important association of human beings. At present the family has no social substitute. He who has not had or does not now have a wholesome family life meets the opportunities and obligations of life seriously handicapped. The more normal he is in his cravings, the greater his sense of loss. The home is not merely an elementary training-place for later life, it is the means by which the material presented by heredity for the making of an individual is shaped into the social structure which we call personality. The fact that the home never turns out a flawless product must not blind us to the fact that he who climbs up through childhood without a quantity of family contacts goes out into life as a result to search for something he desperately needs but cannot find.

In spite of the exaggerated criticism of the family because of the wrong use of its power to influence the life of the child, there is general agreement that the child needs a father and mother, and an affectionate father and mother. It is the other side of the home picture many people do not see. Parenthood is not a penalty that Nature tries to put upon the individual who seeks the pleasures of physical sex; parenthood itself is a normal human need. Parents need the child just as much as the child needs the parents. Being a father or a mother to a child is a social experience that also has no substitute. The parent-child relationship carries with it a source of risk in greater degree than other associations merely because it is so uniquely influential.

Just now we are hearing much about the parents who are unwisely affectionate toward their children and who are constantly trying to keep them from growing out of the dependency that the parents find so delightful. The problem is serious enough to deserve the attention it is receiving, but there is also another angle of the family situation which must not be neglected. The unwelcome child and the child that receives no affection also represent a problem and one not at all less serious than the case of the child smothered by parental affection.

Critics of the family are constantly bringing to our attention persons who find themselves unwilling parents and who refuse to take over any considerable amount of responsibility for their offspring. This condition is common enough to deserve the attack being made upon it, but we are apt to pass unnoticed the opposite kind of predicament. There is a large army of men and women, unmarried or without children, who hunger for parenthood. They are particularly to be found in furnished rooms in the lodging districts of our cities. Many of them are trying to fill the void of their life, which they may consciously appreciate or only unconsciously feel, by adopting various kinds of animals, a cat, dog, parrot, and even a canary bird, and offering them a fellowship which would seem ridiculous, were it not so pathetic. Their more than half-starved cravings for intimate response would find parenthood their happiest and most useful expression. Whether they know it or not, they suffer from the blocking of a great human urge.

Those who without high motive are driven into celibacy or childless marriage are, in the majority of cases, potential parents. Deprived of opportunity to satisfy human impulses that clamor for recognition, they experience at this point a great quantity of personal unhappiness and social irresponsibility.

Much of the trouble with the modern family comes from our not realizing that it must be an end in itself as well as a means. In other words, our artificial way of living betrays many of us into seeking through the home satisfactions that lead us to estimate the value of the home by its power to increase pleasures that can only be secondary to its main purpose and therefore indirect products. A variety of motives impel people to begin family life: sex desire, professional advantage, social distinction, economic security, social pride, and others. The one legitimate reason is the desire to have a full home life and the willingness to learn to love the kind of experiences of close and affectionate contact that distinctively belong to the home. The family has no chance to succeed when people establish it with no thought of enjoying its essential elements, but with the demand that it furnish certain pleasures and nothing else.

If one asks how it is that the family is thus perverted and turned to uses that spoil it as a means of human satisfaction, the answer is not difficult. The conditions of modern life are reflected in the family: materialism, fostered by social suggestion, is sending a multitude of people on a false pleasure-hunt; if they include marriage and parenthood in their programme, they are too apt to insist that these two experiences cater to their life-philosophy. The home came into being as a means of satisfying more genuine and more fundamental human cravings, and when it is turned from its original biological and social purpose, it frequently seems to fail. The institution is then blamed, rather than the false standards of life that attempt to pervert it. Indeed, in the home we find the culmination of harmless influences; the more false ideas of value enter the home, the greater the difficulty of children who come from that home, when later they start new families of their own.

That our modern family in these days of

transition needs attention, if it is to be more socially efficient, no one would deny. Nevertheless, as an institution, it is still responding to human needs; its failures come about from the personality defects and wrong motives of those who agree to establish a home life. Superficially different from the family of the past, it still offers human nature its rarest chance to enjoy the richness of primary contact and the indispensable opportunity to find in parenthood the most socializing and maturing experience given to adults.

The security of the home, therefore, is in human desire. The home has come as a means of satisfying the cravings of men and women for intimate affection and understanding. It is not merely a biological or social necessity: it is primarily an opportunity for profound desires to get satisfaction. The home is not a check but a fulfillment of human impulses.

Even if we could produce children artificially and train them in orphanages, normal men and women would choose to establish homes and have children. In a society where the regulation of sex became the most lax and the conduct of men and women the most individualistic imaginable, most people would choose the conventional marriage and the home. The home provides the best opportunity for the love and fellowship that human nature craves. Here we find the family hazard. We cannot guarantee that any particular couple will find in their living together the satisfactions of comradeship which they crave. Even the ill-mated, by the intensity of their feeling toward family failure, prove the strength of the desire that gives the modern family its security. Adults want family life, even if they often find it difficult to adjust themselves to meet its demands. The great resource of the family lies in the impulses of men and women who turn to it for a means of satisfying their profound cravings for sympathetic comradeship. The future of the family, therefore, is as secure as human nature itself.

To satisfy human needs, the home must change as the life of the people changes; it is not the family of yesterday that is able to satisfy the men and women of to-day or do justice to the children now with us. The family must be modern in the form it takes.

Many good people appear to have lost hope of the family because they have found that it is changing. How could the family remain stationary with everything else moving on? Our houses are different, our interests are unlike those of the past, we have different recreations, and even new features in our government; under such circumstances the family as an institution would be hopeless if it were the only thing that did not change in the midst of a progressing civilization.

The changes that are occurring do not necessarily mean the hampering of the family; instead they provide for the more companionable elements of family life, if only the home is wise enough to use its new resources. There is no necessary relation between the affection of the family and the quantity of cooking done in its own kitchen. As the economic aspects of home life dwindle, there is opportunity for a better kind of home, but it must be built upon the need of human contacts rather than, as in the past, upon the advantages of having a wife to keep house and children to contribute to the family budget as soon as they are equal to doing work. The very fact that the family is no longer, for the mass of people, an economic advantage gives a larger opening for the more personal and more human qualities of home association. If there were no other reason for the existence of the family than its earlier basis of economic necessity, characteristic of the time when the home was fashioned by rural conditions, its future would indeed be hopeless. Fortunately, although it may seldom be a financial help to get married, the desire to have a home of one's own is not by that means lessened. The unfortunate fact is that for many economic pressure may delay the satisfactions they crave and forbid the starting of a family until they have become much too well adjusted to the irresponsibilities of single life.

It is particularly with reference to the children that one sees clearly the great superiority of the home that is coming over that of the past. Not only have children been exploited by child labor, but they have also to a large extent suffered from having their life so thoroughly permeated by the atmosphere of their home. It is not good for a growing individual to be so absolutely under the dominance of the personalities of the father and mother. Now that the family is necessarily limited in its functions, it is more easily prevented from overdoing the service that it has to render to the child. The home used to have no fear of being supplanted as the chief influence upon the developing personality of the child, but it is certainly better for child-life that the home does not have so nearly a monopoly of the impressions that shape the child's character as it once did. Any child brought up in a normal family is bound to have his personality saturated with the flavor of his surroundings. It is not necessary that all the substance of a young life should come out of the family circle.

The rural home was notorious for its power to infect young life with the natural bias of the parents. It is impossible for human nature to escape risk of prejudices. In the past, however, they have been particularly brought to the child by his parents who frequently received their own bias in like manner. As a general rule prejudices do not fix themselves in any individual's personality unless they have soaked in over a long period without the victim's having his suspicions aroused as to their unfairness. Doubtless the parents in the modern family often have prejudices as did their parents, but the more numerous contacts of their child and the greater his recognition, through his larger associations, that the ideas of his parents are not shared by all, the less the danger that he start life handicapped by those stubborn complexes which we call prejudices.

The very fact that the child does not live the larger part of his life within the home encourages in him greater self-reliance. In so far as the family counts less, the individual child is thrown more upon his own resources. Here, of course, there must be the happy medium between absolute neglect and the unrestrained affections which lead so easily to the emotional arrest of the child. Although there are homes that fail to-day, as always there have been, by going either to the one or the other extreme, the natural result of the limitation now placed upon the family in its association with the child by our social life tends toward a family that guides the child without excessively moulding him. Social conditions cannot make parents sensible, but the social situation either encourages or hampers wholesome parenthood. It is certainly true that the changes in our children's environment give the parent of our time the largest opportunity he could ask for to influence his child without discouraging the development of the personality along lines of independence and self-reliance, which the wise American father and mother desire above everything else in their child.

This family policy of developing in their child judgment and self-control is the only one that can be made to work satisfactorily in these days. The old idea, especially with reference to the life of girls, that the family's business is to protect the child at least during the first few years, was never a sound programme and at present it is for most homes absolutely unworkable. The child, whether boy or girl, is almost sure to escape from the clutches of such a family policy and by this escape to show clearly the danger of trying to prepare the child for life in any other way than by the development of his own self-reliance. The normal order is being forced upon the family, even where parents are reluctant to accept the new and better method of preparation for life. The home has merely lost the risk of doing too much: the child has gained an opportunity that seldom denies the chance to grow from within.

From every angle the home, as it ministers to husband, wife, parent, and child, has suffered no loss that enfeebles its power to meet human need. It has surrendered probably for all time some of the enterprises it managed when it was adjusted to the rural type of life. It cannot be a thing apart from the larger social life to the extent it once was, but it is still dominant; it continues its unique possession of the most effective means of satisfying human need as it arises in the yearnings of man, woman, and child.

CHAPTER V

GRINDING DOWN THE MIDDLE CLASS

IF you want to know what is happening to the middle class, study the birth rate. In a recent Associated Press report, Dr. Frederick L. Hoffman, statistician for the Prudential Life Insurance Company, tells us that America's birth rate is at the lowest point in the Nation's history and that there is danger that the finest qualities of the race in intellect, morals, and productivity will be submerged. It is impossible to challenge Dr. Hoffman's statement; the facts are too well established. Startling as the decrease in the birth rate is, its sinister meaning appears in its concentration on the middle class. It is the result of a grinding-down process which threatens this class.

These are the people who are instinctively prudential; they have to be. The well-seasoned middle-class family hesitates to assume risk. It has not reached its position of comfort without struggle. It senses its need of caution if it is to maintain its foothold. Recklessness, particularly economic extravagance, endangers its security. It has no choice; either it must curb its desires or run risk of slipping.

There is no evidence that the falling birth rate is due in large measure to a lessening of physical fertility. The American people are about as vital as they ever have been. It is certainly unfair to regard the falling birth rate as an expression of selfishness, a desire for luxury, or the unwillingness to assume the responsibility of children. Luxury and the desire for freedom may be affecting the birth rate among the wealthy classes, but, so far as the middle class is concerned, prudence is much more influential.

The fact is that children are becoming a family luxury. No middle-class family can hope to have many children without sacrificing actual necessities. No parents are more eager than these to give their children a better start in life than they themselves had. Standards of health and education are so much higher to-day than ever before that middle-class parents have to stretch their resources and industry to the utmost in order to give their children a fair start. Even before the coming of the child, painful problems crop up connected with the expense of expert medical counsel. Nobody understands better than the intelligent middle-class parent the value of the specialist. If the prospective mother intends to follow the advice she has obtained from books and periodicals, or to profit by her own unhappy experience in the past, she soon discovers that the specialist belongs either to the wealthy or to the very poor.

This month a couple of my middle-class friends have had their second child. The man of the house told me a few days ago that it was the last child that would be born in his home, not because he is lacking in affection for children or unwilling to sacrifice comfort and freedom, but because it has been absolutely impossible for him to give his wife and child the kind of care they need. Although his wife's case presented no special difficulties, the hospital bill alone for her first week amounted to nearly half his month's salary. The fact that his wife had been attended by a specialist automatically elevated the hospital charges to a point far beyond his ability to pay. To criticize my friend for employing a

specialist is the same as saying that he ought
not to expect to give his child adequate medical care, for an obstetrician is no more a medical luxury than a surgeon for the operation of
appendicitis.

Occasionally one has to learn the facts by
sad experience, as did one of my neighbors.
This mother of one child saw the need of a
second child to prevent the spoiling of the
first. Her husband, a high-school teacher,
receives a salary just large enough to support
the family in ordinary times, though they live
modestly and spend carefully; so Mrs. B——
went back into teaching for two years, saving
all she cleared, after paying the woman who
took care of her young child in her absence
from home, allowing for the greater expense
of school as compared with house clothes, and
meeting such unusual bills as arose incident
to the health care of the child. With enough
money in the bank to take care of the arrival
of the second baby, Mrs. B—— made up her
mind to get along without an obstetrician and
save that money for the future health needs of
her children, since she felt that with two little
ones to care for she would not be able to get

away from the house long enough at a time to do any more teaching during the years when extra expenses would be most urgent if the children were to have a good foundation for lifelong health. She therefore did not get a specialist to help her prepare for the coming of the new baby. Unfortunately, she made some misstep as the result of her lack of skilled medical guidance and finally had to submit to an operation by a specialist. At the end she found herself without a baby, all her savings gone, facing the probability that she could never have another child. Cheap medical care preceding and at the time of childbirth is about the most risky economy the middle-class family can practice.

It is not merely the cost of having babies that is affecting the birth rate of the middle class. As soon as the child comes, the intelligent parent knows that it must be given a periodic examination by a physician if it is to have a fair start in life. In the past we have not known how much depended upon the physical care of children in their early years. Eyes, ears, throat, posture, development have a foremost place in the list of things that must be looked after and that at any time may require the service of a highly paid expert. The middle class generally has become well acquainted with the ideas of preventive medicine and thoroughly convinced of the fact that in medicine a stitch in time saves nine. It also knows from experience how difficult it is to give a child the needed physical examination and treatment without draining the family purse. Attention that the wealthy can easily pay for, and the poor largely have given them, the middle-class family must get at the cost of real sacrifice, or do without and risk the future welfare of the child.

Such clinics for middle-class people as the one carried on in New York City by Cornell University are pointers that suggest what may sometime be widely done to change this situation; there a moderate charge is made for the services of medical experts, and nobody whose income rises above a specified modest figure need apply for diagnosis or care.

The majority of middle-class parents are conscientious and determined to give their children reasonable physical care. As a result there can be no choice respecting the necessity of having a small family. The expense of one or two children may be safely borne, but the coming of every additional child means just that much more risk that some child may not be given the medical care he needs, because of its expense.

It is when sickness comes that the middle-class family feels most deeply the economic menace of the large family, and among these folk more than three children means a large family. When a parent whose reserve funds must always be slender even though he saves a steady ten per cent of his salary looks at a sick child he has little sympathy with the sentiment recently expressed by one of my medical friends: 'The trouble with you middle-class people is that you don't realize that highly skilled medical service is actually beyond your means. You don't expect to buy a custom-made automobile of the most expensive kind; why should you expect the highest-priced medical service? Frankly, in medicine you should adjust your desires to the service you can afford to pay for, just as you would in buying an automobile.'

No parent can reconcile himself to this idea

that the doctor is just a business man who sells his services to the highest bidder. If having one child rather than two makes it a little more certain that in a time of crisis the sick child can receive the most skilful attendance procurable, is it strange that the most thoughtful parents of limited means should prefer one child to the risk of two?

Any sincere attempt to encourage a higher birth rate among the middle class must look this problem of medical cost squarely in the face, for undoubtedly the present high cost of babies and the expense of providing adequate medical care for children together constitute one of the most significant forces that are now grinding down the middle class by directly influencing the birth rate.

Then there is the problem of education. It is a poor sort of parent who is willing to bring into the world children whom he cannot educate. The more widespread education becomes, the greater is the child's need of it, of course, if he is to have a fair preparation for life. In the ever-mounting cost of living the expense of education leads the procession. Increases in tuition, serious as they are for the average salaried man, represent only a part of the cost of higher education. As the social side of our college and professional school life becomes more and more prominent, the cost of education correspondingly increases. It is true that the students themselves are more to blame for this than the institutions of learning, but the faculties and administrators are by no means free from all responsibility for the present situation. Any college policy that strengthens the intellectual life of the students will tend to lessen the money spent in social activities.

College authorities would make a more heroic effort to curb undergraduates' expenditures along incidental lines if only they came into closer and franker contact with parents. As things now are, our educational machinery is sadly out of gear, in part because the student stands between the college official and the parent. What is greatly needed is a direct interchange of ideas between home and college. One of the first results would be that the parent would understand that the college does not encourage the needless expenditure of money in social activities, while the college would appreciate the need of helping the parent who is trying to check the extravagances of son and daughter, but who cannot succeed without the coöperation of many other parents and the aid of the institution itself.

As things now are, the students who steadfastly try to avoid unnecessary expenses are liable to be thought of as ' lacking in college spirit ' when they refuse to pay five dollars for some banquet, give time and help in getting up and attending numerous parties that demand appropriate clothes and spending money, pay a considerable sum toward the support of the competitive athletics that insure publicity for the institution even if they do not greatly benefit individual students, have their pictures taken at the proper moment, or load up with a bulky and expensive pile of undergraduate literature. So strong is the public opinion of the average body of college students on this score that the student whose most carefully husbanded resources barely suffice for the essential costs of education must have unusual strength of will if he is to stick out four years of patent disapproval from his college mates.

It is rather strange that college faculties should not sense more acutely the seriousness of the financial problem of middle-class parents, for they are themselves in large measure not only members of that class, but very poorly paid members. Apparently they are too busy trying to adjust themselves to a pinching budget to give much thought to the problems of others. Two college teachers were talking the other morning. Said one, 'I believe I shall have to get a police dog; there have been several breaks in our neighborhood recently, and my wife is getting timid.' The second advised, 'It will cost less and work better to put up an electric sign: "A College Professor Lives Here."'

Perhaps it is the logic of our present situation that some of our institutions for higher education should be frankly organized as places for students from middle-class homes. Not only would this check the cost of education for those who chose the proper institution, but also it would have a tendency to classify the student population, so that those choosing college for its social side would go to one kind of institution, while those who primarily sought intellectual training would go to the other. The mischievous fact in all our colleges at present is that we have both types of students, and those socially bent are naturally the ones who are most influential in determining student policies that call for an expenditure of money; the others are too busy with their work to give any large amount of time to college policies.

It may be said that the student can earn his way through college if he has the disposition. Undoubtedly he can help; it is seldom, however, that he can earn a very large part of his expenses, and it is often dangerous for him to try. One who is near the actual conditions of college life finds it appalling that so many of the students who attempt self-support break down physically or do unsatisfactory work in their classes, while others pay for their over-work in later years of ill health or loss of ambition. It is generally an advantage to a student to earn part of his expenses, but the careful parent will wisely hesitate to advise his son or daughter to undertake a large amount of self-support while going through college. Much the same can be said about the student's going in debt for his education. If he has to borrow a large sum of money the handicap he carries as he enters life is so great as to call in question the wisdom of trying to get college training in this way. Of course there are scholarships, but they are neither ample nor abundant, nor are they always wisely distributed, partly because the middle-class student is frequently so sensitive and hesitant in applying for college aid.

The cold facts are that no middle-class parent who lives upon what he earns can expect to see his children educated unless he is willing to restrict himself to two or three children. It is perhaps the sense of insecurity more than anything else that is affecting the birth rate of the middle class. This group of people are by instinct thrifty; the majority of them have been able to arrive at their present place of comfort only by prudence and unremitting diligence. Professor W. I. Thomas has told us that one of the profoundest cravings of human nature is for security. As a group the middle-class people have this craving excessively. It has been unduly emphasized in their attempt to climb to better circumstances or to avoid falling back to the level from which they have come. The time was, perhaps, when the middle class looked upon its children as a means of support or an economic asset. Certainly now the middle-class parent does not consider his child an economic advantage, nor indeed does he want his child as a means of financial security. Now as always he primarily expects to protect himself from future need by means of thrift and safe investment.

No middle-class worker can hope to do much saving unless his family is very small. The little he lays by from year to year and the life insurance that he generally carries furnish little security for his wife and children, if they are left to their own resources by his passing, or for himself and his wife in their old age. The middle-class family lives upon a narrow margin of safety. To be sure, the poor are in a much more precarious position, but they are usually not so sensitive to it. However fond of children the average middle-class parent may be, he must content himself with a small family or menace his security. Some have the courage to risk the future and they are perhaps the wiser of the two groups. The more cautious individual is certain to do otherwise. He will have few children, but solace himself with the belief that he can do justly by them. Though his effort to give his children a better opportunity than he himself had often results in his spoiling them, this is partly because he does not have a large enough family of children to spread his affection upon, and the two or three children that must absorb it all are over-protected by tenderness that is too highly charged with emotion.

The motive that is impelling the middle-class parent to think twice before he has one child, and ten times before he has a second child, is the same motive that is keeping the French birth rate so low. It is the need of keeping the family load from being excessive, for the greater safety of all. In countless marriages of the middle class there is a determination to have no children at all. In this way the *companionate*, the family that exists on the basis of voluntary childlessness, is becoming for many a substitute for a real family.

Public taxation, particularly indirect taxation as it affects the costs of living, influences the birth rate.   The costs of government must, of course, be somehow met by contributions from the citizens; yet we cannot ignore the effect of taxes upon family welfare.   Surely, the home as a social institution has a rightful claim to a consideration as careful as any industrial interest.   Income tax laws, both state and national, recognize the social burden assumed by parents with young children, but the exemptions granted are too small to do much toward equalizing the economic burden of the child-rearing family as compared with the companionate.

Aready experiments are being made in Europe, especially in France, with family subsidies or allowances.   The time when we shall consider such a programme is no doubt distant, but it is not too soon to realize that our tax legislation is never merely a method of getting public funds; it is also a means of adding force to the conditions that are grinding down the middle class.

A society that permits the decrease of the middle class runs greater risk of social explosions.   As the buffer class melts away, the extremes of wealth and poverty come closer together, but without mutual understanding or sympathy. The middle class has always been the group of social mediation. No one would quarrel with social changes that brought all workers up to the grade of comfort characteristic of the middle class. The situation at present is not so much a lifting of those on the lowest economic level as a grinding down of the middle class. It is mostly an elimination, through decrease of births, of a group that feel the economic handicap of children and prefer to give two or three a fair preparation for the competition of life rather than to bring into the world a larger number of children who will be weighted down as a result of the parents' reproductive recklessness. Perhaps the mills of social conditions grind slowly, but so far as the middle class is concerned they grind exceeding fine.

CHAPTER VI

YOUTH SPEAKS

In spite of much talk about the 'Youth Movement' there is in this country nothing that deserves so definite a designation, at least so far as organization is concerned. In Europe also the so-called 'Youth Movement' is more significant as a social trend than as an organization.

We do have a change of attitude on the part of young people that perhaps justifies the characterization of 'Youth Movement.' It is not an entirely new thing, for strain between middle age and youth has, for many generations, been marked by the selfsame gulf and conflict of viewpoint which is so noticeable just now.

The new element is the seriousness of the difference between parent and child and the unprecedented freedom demanded and obtained by American youth to-day. Young people ask right of way over many of the traditions that have been so long-standing as to seem to us who are older firmer than Gibraltar. To a large extent the struggle is hazy, for youth do not clearly know their own desires and their elders are not definite in their prohibitions.

The conflict is largely emotional and issues from the pleasure and self-expression motives that most parents have been assiduously cultivating in their children. The youth movement is in harmony with the infancy and childhood experiences that we have been giving children in large measure in both school and home. It is not only a thing to be expected, but one to be gladly welcomed. It is, however, not without its risks, and if liberty is to be given there is the utmost need that our child-training prepare the individual for his freedom.

Youth likes to exaggerate and also, we must confess, to shock those older. Thus it has always been with young people in the presence of their more habit-bound elders. Doubtless it is a provision of life that youth should not conform easily to the hard-and-fast traditions built upon former experiences and useful in earlier times. It is not strange that there are serious slips. The untoward behavior of some youth is too often generalized and young men and women are catalogued as lacking in all self-discipline. Not merely is this unfair, but it flies hard against facts too obvious to be ignored unless one is blinded by prejudice.

Those who dislike the present-day behavior of our youth are not in doubt whom to blame; it is the parents who are at fault, they tell us. Richly the home deserves an indictment for the plight in which many young people find themselves, yet much of the criticism the home is getting reflects a mistaken notion as to what has happened to the youth of to-day. They have become reckless, so it is said, because of the utter failure of easy-going parents to discipline their children. If our youth are indeed in revolt, a merely negative programme of stringent control would never have warded off the upheaval. Even to try to deal with the growing child on this basis, after the manner of our own parents' methods with us, is bound to be mischievous and may be tragic. It is common experience that those parents are in greatest trouble who have made most heroic efforts to rear their children in an atmosphere of docile submission to discipline in imitation of their own childhood. The family with no pro-

gramme at all, except that of farming out its
irksome responsibilities as soon as it can to
school and state, is also in trouble with its
children, and deservedly so. (No theory of
just letting the child alone gives wholesome
preparation for life. The home has the task
of training the child to meet life by building
up in him self-responsibility and self-control.)

The guilt of the home has not been in its
failure to demand servile obedience of its children, something impossible to accomplish and
disastrous even to try, but rather in its
inability to adjust itself to changing social
circumstances. Unable to meet its own problems, the family necessarily has not been
able to help its children meet theirs. It is not
so new a thing as many people suppose for
youth to revolt. It is the seriousness of the
revolt in our time that makes it something new
in social experience. If one probes any concrete difficulty in the behavior of youth, one
generally discovers at the root a negligent or
backward family life.

Too many of us have attempted to transmit
to the oncoming generation our family traditions, our code of behavior for family mem-

bers, even our ideals governing home life, as if there had been no volcanic changes in our social living together which have made new demands upon family life. The unmodified family which has balked at any adaptation has contented itself with treating its children as if they were lumps of putty to be pressed into traditional moulds by pressure from above. The result was inevitable; such a programme could bring nothing but the revolt of youth who were receiving from outside the home influences that made the archaic family life most dissatisfying. Adult achievements in science, invention, literature, education, and business have undermined and shattered conventional family life just as they have disturbed social habits in other departments of life. The youth have felt the full flush of these sweeping changes and have tried to adapt themselves to the new conditions, while the parents, although at other points they realize the needs of adjustment, have often tried to maintain homes built upon the traditions of the past.

The revolt of youth is an attempt to meet the real needs of the current way of living, unhampered by tradition. Young men and women see the logic of existing social conditions; they feel the imperative command of modern life that they reconstruct their manner of living in order that it may be more in harmony with actual facts than are the ways of their parents. The most conservative and backward parent has encouraged at certain points this onward-looking attitude of his children, for part of what he has trained them to believe is clearly based on fact that can be demonstrated, and is therefore really scientific, at least in quality; while part of what even the most liberal and progressive parent tries to get his children to believe is just what he wants to say and what he has been wishing, and is therefore only self-satisfying dogma.

We parents are not ourselves conscious of the difference in these two types of material that we are forever pouring into the lives of our children. We are made that way. We have had both kinds poured into us and so we can give them to our children without any difficulty, but the children detect the difference; they take part of what we give them, but they call in question our institutions and

our traditions. They would be more frank if
they dared, but we still hold the power and so
they must express revolt in such ways as
prudence dictates.

I was a favored guest at a discussion club
made up of young people, some months ago.
Being the only adult present, my existence was
for the most part ignored, with the result that
I was able to listen in on some unusually frank
talk. I confess that I do not yet know what it
was all about, but I was given one decided
impression: those present were thoroughly
dissatisfied with colleges, churches, newspapers, business, legislation, and pretty nearly
everything else. I had expected plain speaking, but I was surprised and rather shocked at
some of the sentiments expressed with reference to the work of my own profession. College machinery was reversed, for it was the
college professor who was on probation. The
thirty-odd young men and women were not
wild-headed, neurotic agitators. The group
was representative of college life so far as disposition and background were concerned; it
differed from the larger body only by having
a considerably higher intellectual level, for it

contained a disproportionate number of able students who were receiving distinction from the faculty and from their fellow-classmen. Two or three of them were, to be sure, of the erratic type; but the majority were from middle-class homes, of the sort that many delight to call the ' hundred-per-cent American ' type.

In the next ten years we shall get the full force of this revolt because we shall have young people in power. It is not strange that European statesmen are worried about this and are trying ingeniously to prevent it. A striking illustration of the break between parent and child in this generation occurred in a recent political campaign in England, when the premier of that nation stood on one platform as the protector of the Empire, and his son on a radical platform that wanted to wipe out almost everything for which the empire stood.

If our youth are in revolt, they are certainly an unusual type of rebel; they are not much given to the writing of declarations of independence; you do not find them on the street corners shouting out their demands for freedom. Most of them run little risk of

inviting controversy after the manner of Percy
Shelley, who, in his student days, put his radical thoughts in a pamphlet on ' The Necessity
of Atheism," which he mailed to bishops and
others in authority.   They are content rather
to go on their way, doing much as they please
and saying little when rebuked.   They are not
demanding freedom: they are using it.   They
do not ask privileges: they take them.   They
do not defend themselves: they quietly go on
as they please and accept adult interference
with tolerance.   Many of them have neither
doubt nor fear, and it is this undisciplined
confidence that leads them most frequently
into trouble.   It is the strange mixture of
frankness of manner and reticence of motive
that makes the youth movement so baffling
when we try to grasp its meaning, and so
disquieting for those who realize its danger.
Suppose we call modern youth to the stand
as a reluctant witness and demand clear
answers to the questions that come to us when
we try to understand what is happening to
our youth and what they contemplate doing
to us and to the world in which we live.

' Youth, against what are you revolting?'

The first answer we get, and we get it often, is: 'We are revolting against the control of our parents; we like our parents, are glad they happened to be who they were; they are no worse than others, rather better; but we are not going to be under their control in the way they expect. We are decided as to that; we are not any longer the sort of child that used to be. We have settled this consciously and with great determination.'

'What is the matter?'

'Well, we don't accept home training. This does not mean that we dislike our homes or desire to trouble our parents. We had rather do what is expected of us, but in our everyday life we simply cannot conform to all of the restrictions put upon us. We don't need the protection that seemed necessary a generation ago. We can take care of ourselves, and we must meet our own problems in our own way. We cannot explain our situation because our parents and teachers are too rigid in their imagination to see our problems from our point of view. We cannot satisfy both our elders and ourselves, and naturally we prefer to please ourselves.'

' Is that all you are in revolt against?'

' No. All old people are like our parents, and people in these days get old rather early. We are against all traditions of older people, all sorts of traditions, not just those of the home; for out in society we find traditions and customs and rules that are just like what used to be in our homes and we don't accept them when we can help it; we are not in sympathy with them. We are not at all sure these older people are right. We are against parents, traditions, customs: we demand facts, proven principles and the right to experiment.'

' Why are you in revolt?'

' Our parents are too far away from life to be safe guides. They do not know this, for they are of another generation, and the world has changed so rapidly that they are not sensitive to the life that now is, but we are, because we are in it and we know it. We see. The parent cannot see. We do not blame him for it: it is part of his misfortune for having been trained previously; he just cannot sense how different things now are. To be in tune with life as it now is, we have to be a little out of harmony with the kind of life chosen for us by our parents, teachers, and other people. We should not otherwise be able to meet life as it is. We are going to adjust ourselves to our own circumstances; this is the necessity of all life. Our parents and other older friends cannot be trusted. We are sorry for them. They are less sensitive to the actual facts of life than young people because so large a part of their life, as a result of custom and habit, is aloof from actual conditions, segregated, adjusted to other circumstances. They are in part in the world and in part out of the world as it really is, in a sort of reminiscent fiction that reminds us of what they call day-dreaming when it occurs in us.'

' Is that all that troubles you? — that parents do not see life as it is?'

' No. We do not like the rules of society; we do not like the customs. We think they are the result of abnormal influence.'

' What does that mean?'

' It means that the persons who have had much to do with directing the customs, traditions, and even the ideas of the past have not been average people; they have been extraordinary people, exceptional people. It is like

Jerome in the monastery writing a long document telling a distracted mother all sorts of things she must do to train her daughter in the proper way. These so-called idealists are not normal human flesh-and-blood people; they have a great tendency toward asceticism. They are an intellectual type who live in the realm of ideas rather than practice. Having had long-time control of the engine of custom-making, they have brought forth a set of rules that are not good ones for human nature. The result is, we have revolted against them.

' To prove to you that these people are in large measure untrustworthy teachers, we call your attention to the fact that they have never been accepted even by yourself. You have day-dreamed about them and talked about them, but gone on as if they did not exist. Ever so many of these ideas are just the stuff that dreams are made of. We do not intend to be fooled as you have been. Whatever else is true about us, we are going to be genuine; we shall throw overboard everything that is the result of asceticism, prejudice, fear, self-deceit, however deeply embedded in our literature, our preachments, our instruction.

We are probably not so different from what you were, only we are terribly frank and you broke away more gradually, with more concealment and less self-consciousness. If we are very different, it is because we are more genuine, have our eyes open in a way you did not have. We see the facts clearly and are going ahead on the basis of fact. That is going to be characteristic of our attitude in any case.'

'But don't you value experience? Don't you suppose human nature has learned anything from being on the earth? Haven't parents and other older people anything to contribute from their years of living?'

'Yes, we believe in experience, provided it is ours, but we are not going to take yours, because we cannot trust you; we do not know how honest you are or how clear-thinking you were when you had it. We are going to learn our own truths from our own experience; we cannot accept yours. You ought to be sure what is the wise thing to do with life, but you know, yourself, that your great-grandfather's experience was not trustworthy and we do not think yours is, because you have never taken a perfectly honest and critical and frank attitude toward your experience; you have always let your judgment be colored by feeling.

'Experience has its value and also its danger. We know a great many people are not as sound as when they were younger, although they have had more experience. We know that many of our officials and teachers have lost more than they have gained by their experience. They have become narrow, sometimes mean-spirited, trivial, sometimes fussy; they have become arrogant, in love with distinction. We think that experience is just about as dangerous as it is valuable. We dare not trust it by itself. If we are going to trust experience, we must first analyze the person who has had it; if it has made him meaner and smaller, we would rather have him without it. Older people do not recognize that they sometimes lose by just growing up. They call it maturity, development; but it is like a ship that starts out with a large cargo and throws it overboard gradually to lighten ballast, so that it enters harbor with little of value.'

'What are you getting, young people? You must be getting something; you seem to be greatly in love with life.'

' We are getting something human nature loves; we are going to get more of it. We have a word — it is our word — that explains what we are getting out of life; it has never been used so much before: we are getting *thrill* out of life.'

' What is that?'

' It is what you call scientifically *stimulation*. We are very frank about our demand for thrills. We are so frank about it that we are shocking. We say things to one another that put our attempts for thrill on a perfectly conscious and unconventional standard that would certainly at times almost frighten our parents. For instance, in our dancing we tell one another just exactly what we are doing. We are dancing for thrills and we love it for just that reason; dancing is more thrilling than ever before. Unless we can have that, we don't want to dance. Don't you think human nature ought to get out of life all the stimulation it can?'

' Is that all?'

'No. In order to have thrill, we must have adventure, a peculiar type of thrill that carries with it the element of uncertainty and gamble. In addition to orthodox thrill we must have some adventure. The trouble with you people is, you have not provided opportunity enough for us to get adventure. We have had to find new, unorthodox ways. We must have excitement; we cannot live without it. If you must know what we are getting out of life, we are getting thrills and having adventure. Our comrades in Germany who flock about the country, especially on Sundays, have all sorts of restrictions, self-imposed, and no others; recognize no church, no home. They are doing the same sort of thing only in a different way; they are after adventure. We love it as the gypsies do. We have been caught by it and it means a great deal to us.'

It is with reference to the future of society that the adult has misgivings about the youth movement. If the revolt of youth is a new species of wild-oats sowing, to be followed by a settling-down to the task of serious living after the manner of aristocratic young men of some decades ago, then we need not be too much concerned. But if it is something else—? That is our fear. Suppose we call youth back on the stand and cross-examine it as to its purposes for the future.

' Now, young person, what will you do when you get this life in your hands? You will finally get it by the natural process of the disappearance of the rest of us. What will you have?'

' First, we are going to have freedom, that is our cornerstone; and then we shall have as much else as possible. Of course we know the things you will say about it: "It is not so easy to have freedom as it is to talk about it"; "What will you do when one person's freedom interferes with another's?" and "Unlimited freedom spells hubbub." We recognize the obstacles, but we shall have all the freedom we can. Another thing we are going to have is buoyancy. We are not going to have you people with long faces; we are going to have expressions of buoyancy at any rate. Eat, drink, and be merry—especially be merry. We are going to have less exploitation. We don't think much of the world you have. It has too much exploitation. You call it Christian. We don't think it is. Strong and fortunate people are unfair to weak ones. We do not know how we are going to solve all these problems, but we are going to have very much less exploitation than you have, and as a result we are going to have less separation. We are going to have one big democratic class. We do not hesitate to make love and marry outside our class. We do not hold to your scheme at all. We do not believe the things you teach. Our programme is freedom, buoyancy, less exploitation, and much less separation. We agree with Robert Burns,

> " *It's comin' yet for a' that,*
> *That man to man, the world o'er*
> *Shall brothers be for a' that!*"

' What are you going to do with your children? Are you going to have a break with them, as we have with you?'

' Some of us are not going to have any children; we ought not to; we are not fit to have them. If we have children, it will be because we want them and have a right to have them. We shall let science handle this problem for us. We are not going to have children merely to perpetuate the race. There will be enough who wish children to take care of the race.'

'Some of you will have children; what are you going to do with them?'

'We are going to give them just what we have ourselves, only more of it, more freedom, more buoyancy, more democracy, and most certainly more thrills.'

This clear and definite statement of what our youth are driving at discloses the source of their programme; our youth are not the victims merely of family neglect: they are the logical products of present-day social life. Take their craving for thrill. If Professor James could describe the career of the baby in his day as 'an introduction to one big, blooming, buzzing confusion,' what words are adequate to express what happens to the baby in these days? He literally comes into the world surrounded by jazz music, the automobile horn, and the snarl of the loud-speaker; everywhere about him is an atmosphere of haste, movement, tension, and restlessness. He is overwhelmed by the multitude of things thrust upon him. Snatched from the cradle long before he can walk, he is transported through noise and dust on long automobile trips. He is trained to crave thrill, and the kind of thrill materialism furnishes. By the time he leaves childhood he has become satiated with all the thrilling experiences that parents are willing to furnish, and to satisfy his habit of craving he now climbs over the fence of family prohibition to investigate the possible thrills in new pastures hitherto unexplored.

In like manner the child is charged with a hunger for what he calls 'freedom,' which to the adult means ' license.' In the average home he is given as much luxury as the family purse allows, and even the poorest of families now enjoys luxuries; then he is left much to himself, his freedom broken only intermittently by occasional punishment from parents who vent their ill temper or fatigue upon him, or who hasten to punish him because his doings have become too troublesome to withstand or are likely to attract the unfavorable attention of neighbors.

On the other hand, when the child steps from the home into the school, he finds everything in utter contrast to his family life; instead of freedom, all is cut and dried, standardization and supervision face him from every side. He receives a mental testing, the results of which may not only prescribe his treatment in the school, but in the minds of his instructors catalogue him for all time, and determine the standard to which he has to live up — or live down, as the case may be. His out-of-the-school activities are intruded upon by adult supervision, for purposes of development, economy, and efficiency. The teacher is skilled in the art of suggestion and manipulation, and the child may not sense the coercion that is put upon him. In the vocabulary of school theory the word, *coercion,* does not appear; it is replaced by *supervision* and *direction.* If the schools of a generation ago had sharper discipline and more regulations, they also to a much greater extent let children do their tasks without interference. Present-day pedagogy has an itch for meddling; it makes some children docile and the rest eventually rebels.

The child receives in the home a taste of erratic freedom and in the school too little chance for spontaneous self-expression, even though he does have enormous self-expression in the form prescribed by the school strategists. Suggestion and prescription, even when skillfully manipulated, are merely more subtle kinds of coercion. One does not have to go far afield to discover the social causes of the modern youth's desire for freedom from regulation. After enjoying the home life which has given him a taste of irresponsible license, he is driven into the herding process of the school, which is usually mechanical and frequently finical. Irresistibly his life moves toward a freedom his training has given him little preparation to use rationally.

It is not strange that we find theories of a more democratic social life in the youth movement programme; this is merely the logical application of the teaching they have received from adults. We are reminded from time to time that our government was based upon the Constitution and not the Declaration of Independence. The fact is obvious, but it is equally true that American sentiment has more largely issued from the first document. Even if we do not wish to practice all of the tenets of social democracy, we at least love to talk about them. Youth are more apt to practice sentiment because they are free of the prejudices of those that have become hard-boiled as a result of the competitions of life. Even if the social ideals of our youth are hazy, they are genuine, and it is at just this point that we find the greatest gulf of separation between the youth and their elders.

Buoyancy is the very essence of youth. In the past the sentiments of youth have been largely inarticulate, and so buoyancy has had a small place in the philosophy of life and the code of conduct. The difference merely is that under modern conditions youth are able to contribute their attitudes to the social programme.

Thus the youth movement throws in high relief the social influences at work in our adult world. We older people are partly the products of the social life of yesterday; our youth are the first fruits of the social conditions we have ourselves created in this modern world.

CHAPTER VII

HOME UNDER THE MICROSCOPE

THE home is to be called on the carpet: the summons comes from science and there can be no evasion. The school, the college, the church have faced their critics; now it is the turn of the home. Not only has it been demonstrated that many of the troublesome problems that adults face come about as the result of unfortunate childhood experiences, but that the home is more often to blame than people in the past have realized.

It used to be thought a very simple matter to spot the bad family. The home that neglected its children and let them roam around the streets, that quarreled or was drunken or shiftless, such a home was bad: all the others were good. Recent science, particularly psychiatric science, has knocked this easy philosophy of family life into a cocked hat; now we know that a home cannot be pronounced good merely because its parents are respectable citizens, its lawn always well-cut in summer, and its back yard free from rubbish. We have discovered that children can be seriously taken care of by their parents, brought up on a health diet, given every facility for education, and still receive a childhood injury, perhaps unknown to the parents, which makes a happy, successful life more difficult than it ought to be, or even impossible.

Science has placed the home under the microscope, and as a result we are beginning to have adequate knowledge of the meaning of good family life. Science, however, is not at variance with common sense, for what it is now saying has always been more or less recognized by those who were thoughtful in their judgments of human behavior.

There are people who presume that, since the home no longer does nearly so much work as it once did for the children, its influence upon child life is practically negligible. This is a great mistake, and the findings of science demonstrate more and more that, so long as the home has the child largely under its thumb during his first years, its part in the shaping of human personality will necessarily be greater than that of any other social institution. It is not strange that the home should be able to do so much to the child to hurt or to help him in ways that influence him all his life. Those who are expert in training horses and dogs have long realized that the disposition of the animal is largely fixed during the first few months of its life and to no small degree determined by the treatment that it receives from those who have it in charge. It is just the same with a child, only more so: he is more easily harmed and helped than an animal, because he is so much more sensitive, and whatever is done to him has a more lasting effect, since it becomes intertwined with so many different sides of his life that it can neither be pulled out nor entirely suppressed.

We do not put the home under the microscope merely to discover how it affects child life, for sometimes the bad thing about the home is not what it is doing to the children—we must not forget that in many of our modern families there are no children at all—but the consequences of the family life upon one of the adults. It is true that for quick and deep impressions upon personality the home shows its power most when we study its effect upon the child; in the case of adults what it does may be more gradual and not so easy to detect, but over a series of years it shows itself almost equally mischievous.

The fact that the family must be a wholesome association for all of its members discloses in how many ways home life can fail, and it is not surprising under such circumstances that we are now having such a tremendous sweep of criticism with reference to home life. The more we trace the causes that influence persons, the more certain we are to go back to the home as the chief starting-point of the majority of difficulties that hamper individuals in their living and vex society.

One of the bad families that often pass among the thoughtless as ideal is the family that devours the personality of one of its members. Here is such a family. A very wealthy and ambitious student became infatuated with a department-store clerk. She was a clever girl and pretty, who had had little opportunity and had gone to work early, finishing only the grammar school. Almost by instinct, the young woman seemed to realize that her only chance to hold her lover in her power

after marriage was to perpetuate the relationship of their courtship; so in a most ingenious
way she began as soon as she was married to
make demands upon him that kept him busy
trying to meet her needs. In the honeymoon
days this was most natural and he fell into the
rôle assigned him without any hesitation. She
contrived to keep him playing the part he had
taken over and when the first child appeared
she found an ally to help her in her strategy.
Eventually the young man, who had once been
studious, had no time to read or study except
late at night when the mother and child were
in bed. He had long since given up any serious interest in public affairs, which at one
time had fascinated him when he had looked
forward to some sort of public career. This
family still goes on functioning at a level that
one would call a honeymoon fixation, but now
habit has come to the wife's aid and his years
of servitude have taken from the husband all
thought of maintaining his own life, for with
a pathetic resignation he takes it for granted
that his predicament is that of most married
men. As the child has grown, she has also
assumed that ' Daddy ' was a sort of higher

servant, and in trying to meet the whims of both mother and child his personality has melted away about as rapidly as October snow passes in our Eastern States.

Another bad family that often escapes the criticism it deserves is the family that warps personality. This process is so subtle that the usual observer has no understanding of what a perverse influence the family is exerting, but most of us know well at least one family of this sort. A young country boy, well-disposed but not overmuch endowed with intellect, given only the inadequate training of the one-room schoolhouse in a little Vermont town, was fed in his early years by his father repeated doses of religious prejudice. The father had formed an intense dislike for one of the local churches, and the denunciation of this particular body of religious believers had become his meat and drink. In season and out of season, at every opportunity he was ready to tirade against the church he so much disliked. The little boy heard him and took him seriously. With the father the whole matter was a sort of intellectual hobbyhorse, which he enjoyed riding. His friends had learned to mix a grain of salt with his rabid utterances, but not his child, who grew up to think that the most dangerous thing in all the world was the influence of this much-discussed denomination. As soon as he became an adult, he continued the father's crusading, but did not content himself with mere words. Whenever he could he injected his tenets into the life of his community and was the cause of bad feeling that finally developed into a religious feud that divided the social groupings of the village and countryside and entirely spoiled the associations of a delightful rural place.

Another type of bad family is that which we can well call the shut-in family. We have all heard the psychiatrist criticize the shut-in personality that is unwilling to cope with the realities of life. We can also have a shut-in family. This family concentrates all its interest upon its own members; it lives in the community, but is not of it. Its indifference to other people is like a stone wall that cannot be scaled. When it has children, they play only among themselves. I was told recently of two girls in high school who were not permitted to have any playmates or anything beyond a mere speaking acquaintance with any other children.

In a Western suburb not long ago lived a family of this kind. It was never known to take the slightest interest in any of the community enterprises. Once, when somebody had the courage to ask for a contribution for the local hospital, she was told frankly by the man of the house that he was interested neither in hospitals, schools, nor anything else that had to do with the community life; his interest was absolutely confined to his family and his place of work. He maintained a beautiful home, but was always fussing with his neighbor's children because they dared step on his lawn or touch his hedge as they passed by. Indeed, he seemed to think that everybody was seeking a chance to prey upon his property, and when out from the city on holidays, Sundays, and late afternoons, prowled around his premises as if trying to find some culprit whom he could threaten with arrest for daring to invade his precincts. The consequences were inevitable: he soon became a marked man to all the children of the street; hated by his neighbors because of his criticism of their children, he and his wife and one child were in perpetual disturbance. He grew conscious of his unpopularity and after a few years of stubborn resistance moved elsewhere. His neighbors were interested in following his career, and they soon learned that he was repeating his experiences in the new community, and, indeed, was saying to his fellow-workers at his place of business that the new neighborhood was no better than the old. One of his former neighbors slyly remarked that it was not strange that he was unhappy in his new home, when he had been obliged to carry himself along in the moving. A shut-in family is bound to be a social problem, particularly because of its influence upon its children.

A maiden lady undertook to bring up the orphaned children of a couple that had been friends of hers. Being of middle age and set in her ways, afflicted also, it later appeared, with an exaggerated inferiority complex, the would-be benefactress of the five children withdrew more and more from direct contact with the world so that her authority over her wards should meet with as little competition as possible. One after another, church, school, and neighbors were seen to be holding out conflicting fingers of authority over the growing children, so that she had to save her sense of her own dominance by retreating from the boundaries of the rival powers. Church was sneered at, school given up and the children taught at home by herself, and finally the hold of public opinion as expressed in neighborliness was evaded by a continual moving about from pillar to post, stopping only in outlandish or isolated places, so that the children could form no ties of friendship with others of their own age or come under the close scrutiny of any of their elders save their domineering guardian. After the first year household help of any kind was taboo, as it was found that from maid or laundress the children gleaned ideas that minimized the importance of the precepts of their devoted foster-mother. The elder children soon reached the point where they must step out of the narrow confines of their home to take up vocational training, but the two youngest ones felt the cramping repression of this extreme form of shut-in family life for many years; and the baby of the family, having spent her tenderest years in this rigid environment, developed pronounced shut-in traits.

The family that fights has always been a notoriously bad family; the new science helps us to understand the difficulties of such homes by getting at the causes of the incompatibility, which is often due to a feeling of inferiority on the part of one of the members of the family and shows itself in a constant jealousy. There is an unfounded opinion commonly held by people that jealousy is merely a matter of inheritance and that there cannot be any explanation of why one child is jealous and another not so. In such cases it is usually easy to discover that the jealousy had a definite origin as the result of some childhood experience and that oftentimes the parent himself was to blame for what occurred, because he praised one child at the expense of the other; or perhaps his treatment of one child has shown a favoritism which the other child has felt deeply and resented, so that in time the slighted child has developed a chronic state of jealousy.

One of the most remarkable cases of this

sort that I ever came across was one in which an older sister insisted that her younger sister should not marry before herself. As A, the older girl, did not have very much opportunity to win the favor of men, it did not seem as if B, the younger sister, would have any hope of matrimony; B was kept in a state of submission by an hysterical tendency in A that was most alarming to the parents and all the other members of the family; when A could not have her way she became sick, and she always became sick when she saw that her younger sister, who was exceedingly popular, was getting interested in some individual man. As a result the younger sister would drop her acquaintanceship, and the whole situation in time became so conscious that even the friends of the older girl knew she was likely to be sick if B continued to receive the attention of some man who was beginning to get interested in her; this was sufficient to make B drop her male friend. When the more popular sister was remonstrated with by some of her friends, she said that, having once seen her sister in a serious breakdown, she had made up her mind that, though she might never marry, she would not become seriously interested in any man until her sister had married. Eventually the elder sister did marry, but the younger one never has.

One of the worst families is a home that gives almost no real sympathetic fellowship to its children. It is almost as bad as an orphanage, because in an institution children at least have fellowship with other children of their own age, but in some of our families of only one or two children, where the parents are busy, especially when the mother is engaged in some outside career, the children are not only lonely, but are actually destitute of the right sort of human fellowship.

Here is the case of a family that denied its children their birthright of fellowship. The man, a doctor, married simply because he felt it was necessary for him to have a wife. He chose one of his relatives who seemed likely to be a good housekeeper and as good a mother as any one he knew, and it was necessary for him to have somebody that was responsible to keep his house, that he might start on his life-work. He gave all his thought and most of his time to his vocation. The mother did well by the children in their early years, but, because of the large family she had and the exacting demands put upon her by her husband in her housekeeping, it became increasingly difficult for her to give to the children the attention they needed. It was not strange that in such a home there soon developed a very serious problem of delinquency. The eldest boy began to go about to the lower places of amusement, fell into bad company, and began to steal. When his thefts became known, the father heaped blame upon him, but the mother was more discerning as to who was really to blame. His father could do nothing with the boy, who set himself upon the pathway that led straight to State prison. Even yet, people who know the family wonder why it is that such a respectable father should have had so disreputable a child. The boy has no doubt, any more than the mother, as to who was to blame, and he hates his father with a religious zeal. The other children also show to a lesser degree the neglect of the father, with the exception of the youngest. At the suggestion of a social worker who had investigated the case of the eldest boy, this child was given by the father a reasonable amount of fellowship. The result seems to have demonstrated, as the worker believed, that the real difficulty was the lack of comradeship between father and son.

Children need their parents, but it is equally true that parents need their children. Nothing pays interest like the fellowship of child with parent. Nobody can do his full duty toward his children until he learns that the supreme privilege of a parent is to enjoy his children.

Another family that makes trouble is the one that stunts the growth of its children. This is one of the most common difficulties of modern American family life. A child, to be normal in his social contacts, must be led out of his dependency upon his father and mother, particularly upon his mother, into a wider fellowship. There are parents who do not want their children to grow up. They are unwilling to have their child *hurt* by the natural process of growth. As soon as the child's impulses lead him to look outside the family nest, they put every obstruction possible in the way of his growth; they attempt to mould him in a state of dependency by prolonging his infantile reactions. The consequences are that out in life are a multitude of people who, because they were hampered in their natural effort to develop self-reliance, remain infantile in their reactions, although to the outward eye they are fully matured adults. Infantile in their attitudes, they are exceedingly sensitive, and when hurt by the rough contacts of the world of business and social affairs, standardized to the needs of the mature, they express their feelings like children; they are easily angered, quick to become jealous, instinctively suspicious, and often try to obtain a sense of importance by self-deceit and boasting. Wherever they go they make trouble; they are especially menacing when they obtain power as they sometimes do by inheritance of a family business. They are most unreasonable in their demands upon their workers, and love a quarrel because it gives them a chance to show their power. No type of personality leads to so much restlessness, when given authority over workers, as the child who has not grown up. The infantile personality is particularly attracted to lines of work that give power by making one part of a powerful organization. Thus we find teachers who choose their profession because of infantile characteristics, since they can obtain opportunity to command inferiors and be protected by the system to which they belong.

One high-school principal, who was excessively touchy and high-handed in his dealings with students and staff, could not rise to the higher positions his keen mind and fine training fitted him for, because he had no more control over his emotional outbursts than a four-year-old; when crossed or not accorded the deference he craved, he would indulge in the most biting sarcasm or even resort to out-and-out rudeness in a blind effort to ridicule and humiliate his annoyer. The flush of anger or embarrassment on his victim's face was to him like a red flag to a bull; he went on and on, heaping insult on insult, until he could gloat over the work of his tongue; but cool indifference quelled and frightened him so that he retreated within his shell of good manners and let a calm opponent severely alone at any cost. Good administration was an impossibility under so flickering a personality, and a small town held the services of this brilliant man at a very small salary. The explanation of his infantile management of his emotions lay in the over-solicitous devotion of his cultured and wealthy parents, who had tried to make up to their youngest child for what he missed by being cut off from the ordinary joys of boyhood on account of the delicacy of his health in early life: too zealous catering to his pleasure became a habit with them, continued long after his health had established itself, and demanded by him now of the world-at-large since his parents were no longer able to grant the wishes of his manhood.

It is high time that science gave critical attention to the family. By so doing, it is not attacking the family as some mistakenly suppose; it is undertaking the one thing now most needed to make possible better and happier home life. The family has been protected by a common feeling that it is too sacred for investigation. Only families that could not function because of vice or poverty or bad mating have been turned over to the social case worker for study. As a consequence of our social attitude, the family has been permitted to lag behind other institutions, saved by its tradi- tional and easy-going self-satisfaction from searching criticism and scientific investigation.

Nothing in these days can be more perilous socially than an archaic family. The family cannot keep up if no effort is made to dis- cover its failures. It is contrary to facts that stick right out in every country neighborhood and city block to assume that all who mean well are bound to be good husbands, wives, or parents. As matrimonial ventures and child- hood experiences become more hazardous as a result of our eight-cylinder civilization, it will become increasingly clear that training for marriage and parenthood rather than a false confidence in the sufficiency of the pair- ing and parent instincts must be the basis of wholesome home life.

CHAPTER VIII

PARENTS WHO HAVEN'T GROWN UP

WHEN is a parent not a parent? If you have ever tried to help straighten out a family difficulty you will not find the question hard to answer. A parent is not a parent when he still remains a child. No adult is more mature than his emotions. If, in spite of years and experience, a parent persists in dealing with life in the emotional ways of his childhood, he is an adult only in bulk. The savage knew this and treated men of this type as ' boys not yet made men.' That we have parents who refuse to grow up is one of the recent discoveries of psychology and sociology. Of course there have always been such parents; the difference is that now we are beginning to understand what their difficulty is.

Men and women in their emotional life find growing up hard. Like Peter Pan, they don't want to grow up, at least not in that part of their life where wishes start and feelings are free. Adulthood means discipline, self-control, judgment, responsibility, and justice. These are all irksome to human nature, they make such demands upon it and challenge so frequently the desires upon which the heart is set. In his wishes and passions and his moods the immature adult behaves very much as he did when he was a child. When feeling runs strongly and throws aside for the moment caution and sanity, he falls back into the tantrum and emotional exploitation of his early years.

Jealous because of the attention shown his wife at a dance to which he has escorted her, he sneaks home early, throws himself on his bed without undressing, and refuses to speak or move when his perturbed spouse rushes in, expecting to find that he has fallen suddenly ill; all night he keeps his pose of rigidity and for the next two or three days cannot be inveigled into saying a word while within the doors of his own house; finally he blurts forth his tale of woe and tries to make his wife promise never to go to another dance. If she gives in to this, he will use similar methods to coerce her into playing up in other ways to his inflamed sense of self-esteem.

If the immature member of the marriage partnership happens to be the wife, tears and headaches, with frequent vituperation, are perhaps her commonest substitutes for the name-calling and sulking of the cry-baby moods she has carried over from childhood.

Of course all of us are childish at times in our fumbling attempts to do what we set ourselves to do. In the grip of anger, fear, jealousy, or hate our reactions are not very different from those of the child mastered by the same emotions. Experience provides a cloak with which we conceal somewhat our emotional immaturity, but the covering is thin and the deception works chiefly with ourselves.

Have you ever known intimately any adult who never takes an excursion back into the magic and freedom of infantile emotional reactions? The infantile type of adult is not satisfied to indulge in an occasional visit to the land of emotional abandonment; if he possibly can, he refuses to leave it at all, and clings to his self-centered and irresponsible ways of dealing with people and situations. He knows what children do not and does what children cannot, but if you lay bare his emotional life you find him still a child.

The adult with immature emotions is much too canny not to try to hide his childishness. He knows that he is expected to grow up, that society frowns upon emotional immaturity. His fault, however, defeats his efforts to cover up his weakness.

This emotional arrest which characterizes the adult who holds fast to infantile tendencies shows itself most clearly in the business of parenthood. The defect of the parent permeates the life of the growing child at every point and becomes an obstruction to wholesome development. In his struggle to free himself from his entanglements, the child frequently goes through a conflict whose scars he will always carry.

The parent who is himself a child storms and bosses, praises extravagantly, and in the same measure scolds, teases, hugs, spanks, and ignores his offspring in whirlwind pace, until the only thing the youngster is sure of is he never knows what is coming next, but that there will be plenty of it. Exaggeration and briefness of mood characterize youth, but they are practically harmless there: joined to the strength and authority of age in its contacts with youth they are harmful enough; driven by the immature parent's desire to perpetuate a relationship which gives him so much opportunity for the indulgence of his emotional caprices, they do more harm than can be gauged.

The rapidly advancing science of conduct, therefore, has been forced to recognize as one of the perils of young life the emotional immaturity of the parent. Three sciences particularly have been gathering innumerable illustrations of the hazard the child faces in his attempt to unravel the mysteries of human behavior when one or both of his parents are emotionally immature. Psychology with its modern effort to understand human conduct, psychiatry with its practical problems of re-education for those who think themselves mentally sick, and sociology, in so far as it deals with concrete human situations—these sciences find again and again that human development is hurt and the weakness of one generation is transmitted through contact and suggestion to some form of weakness in the next, because of the infantile character of parents.   In fiction this has never been better portrayed than in Butler's ' Way of All Flesh,' whose theme represents a tragedy concerning which science is now getting detailed knowledge.

In our large cities we have habit clinics for young children.   The parent who finds his child too much for him can bring the troublesome offspring to a clinic specialist and get counsel that will make the family life once again endurable.   These habit clinics are really more for the parents than for the children, since it is usually discovered that it is the parents who must first be given new attitudes and new understanding or the child problem will remain hopeless.

The fact that the clinic must stress the child-side of its function shows the way adult emotions must be catered to, for a sensible parent would take for granted his share of responsibility for a child problem.   Many of the parents most likely to need help would not visit the clinic at all if it were known as a habit clinic for children *and* parents.   The intelligent parent realizes that at times every parent and child needs disinterested counsel, which can best be obtained from the experienced scientist.

One of the most common problems uncovered in the parent at the clinic is that of emotional immaturity, and the task of the specialist is to find a way to develop the parent by using the opportunity presented by the difficulty which the parent is having with his child. No diplomat has greater need of tact, shrewdness, and insight into human nature than the family adviser who is forced to deal with a childish parent who, through his own failings, has created a family situation so serious that assistance has to be sought. This is because the parent disguises his immature emotions by all sorts of reasons that at least hide from him his own failure. This is the familiar process of rationalization, which the practical psychologist and sociologist are forced to recognize in almost every difficulty of adjustment. Human nature is forever trying to get its emotional satisfactions with a clear conscience, and so it dresses up its unworthy motives in a fiction of good purposes.

No one has so great a chance to nourish

self-deceit as the parent. The child has to take what is meted out to him, and if the parent does the unwise thing for his own gratification he can cover up his motives by insisting that he is doing it for the good of the child. To see this working in concrete cases would be most amusing were it not such a desperately serious thing for the persons concerned, especially for the child.

The adjustment of mother and daughter in a family came to my attention repeatedly. Sometimes the daughter asked for counsel, sometimes the mother, and once or twice they both came together—this in itself being somewhat extraordinary. This young student persisted in unusual infantile habits that constantly showed in her college career, especially in her fraternity life, to the discomfort and even disgust of her comrades, as when she whined in a near-to-tears voice over the minor difficulties of life, or cried over a misplaced slipper as she was dressing for a dance. Her childish lack of self-control in trifles of this sort was no secret, but was widely known on the campus. The least annoyance, and she began to weep or indulged in an emotional outburst in no way different from that of a six-year-old child. Yet this young woman was intellectually alert and efficient. Physically well made, with a face of strong features and a clear, penetrating voice, she made a favorable first impression.

After graduation from college, against the will of her mother, the daughter took a position that carried her away from close contact with home. This step met with great opposition from the mother, who came to me to enlist my support for her plan to keep the daughter at home. It was necessary to explain with some frankness the risk the mother ran of losing the daughter's sympathies altogether by the course she persisted in following. Confronted by the probability that if she hampered her daughter too much she might lose all control, the mother reluctantly withdrew her objections. Then came the inevitable marriage engagement, with an intense family upheaval. Again the mother was made to see the selfish and childish character of her hostility, and its serious danger of becoming a permanent basis of separation.

I was not surprised, several months after

the marriage, to have a visit from both the daughter and the mother. The daughter came first with a tale of woe which showed that her infantile habits were beginning to make trouble between her and her husband. The young woman had considerable self-knowledge and, recognizing her problem, she was eager to have counsel as to how she could help herself. A few days later the mother appeared at my office. She hardly knew what she wanted. First, she expressed her regret that her daughter had ever married; her child was the kind that ought never to have married, and it was clear that her marriage was a failure. The mother could suggest nothing that could be done to save the situation. When she was asked to tell frankly whether she was hoping the marriage would be a failure and what she thought she could gain if it so turned out, she found herself face to face with a great moral crisis. Of course she wanted her daughter to be happy. It was hard to think that she could be happy in an attachment with another human being. This was plain jealousy, childish jealousy, and the mother had to be told again that this was the flaring up of the same

menacing attitude which she had shown for
so many years. She also had to be told clearly
that, if she used her influence in any way to
perpetuate the difficulty of the two young people, the daughter would surely turn against
her as the despoiler of her happiness. She
had sense enough to see that this was true;
and, keeping her hands off, she was amazed
at the rapid progress the new family made in
adjusting itself to the requirements of marriage happiness.

The mischief is that parenthood, since it
has the best opportunity to affect young life,
provides the most dangerous conditions for
the child when a parent maintains childish
emotions. The child is so open to the influence of the parent, so ill-prepared to discrimi-
nate between the best and the worst of the
parent's attitudes, that his life is warped in
the early years before he has the contacts with
the outside world that would otherwise show
him his parent's weakness.

Family life is so intimate that it provides
a freedom of expression which can be found
nowhere else. The parent still a child, therefore, finds in the home an opportunity for the

expression of emotional reactions that he would not dare show elsewhere. Indeed, the exigencies of life have frequently forced maturity in the other relationships, but at home one can be oneself, which often means that one can be one's childish self, knowing full well that there can be no serious criticism, as there certainly is in business and professional relationship if one gives way constantly to childish motives.

If the outside public recognizes that there is something wrong with the family, the blame is more likely to fall upon the child than upon the parents, for it is taken for granted that the parents wish the happiness of their children. This is a great fallacy, at least if it is assumed to be true of all parents. Many parents wish the happiness of their children only as long as that happiness is in agreement with their own purposes. The child represents an outlet for their emotional immaturity, which they by no means wish to lose. If the child goes their way, all is good; if he goes his own way— which not infrequently is far the better way since it is more in harmony with his real needs for growth—nothing is good. A struggle ensues, in which parental authority is used with drastic force, until the child is driven into conduct that seems to prove his evil make-up, which the undiscriminating outside world has taken for granted all through the contest.

This explains why children brought up in supposedly excellent homes sometimes do not turn out as expected. Such homes often have good habits and strict discipline, to which the children conform. They obey, however, only because they are forced to; they follow the line of least resistance. Their conformity is merely from the outside. Along with their habit of action grows an increasing inner hostility to the régime which they have to follow. As a result, they also have an emotional habit of protest, altogether different from their outward behavior. What the observer sees is but the shell; the substance is out of all sympathy with the home conditions. Naturally, at the first opportunity, the child revolts, throws aside all his training, both good and bad. Then those who are acquainted with his manner of life in early childhood wonder how so bad a character can come from so good a home, and express skepticism with reference to the influence of home life, saying, perhaps, ' Some children are inherently bad; it makes little difference what you do. X is a good illustration. No child was more properly brought up, and see what has become of him.'

One of the common forms of emotional arrest is a father or mother fixation. The child dependent upon the parent is carried over into adulthood without ever accepting self-responsibility. He is always talking about his parent, allowing the parent's ideas to dominate his life. Usually the son is fixed upon his mother, the daughter upon her father. This form of emotional immaturity is forever causing jealousy and friction in the home.

A business friend once invited me to stay at his home when I was speaking in his neighborhood. I knew him slightly and had heard that his business career had been disappointing. When I entered his home the reason for his lack of success was not difficult to discover. His wife, who had just recovered from one of her intermittent attacks of neurasthenia, began talking of her father and comparing others with him, to their disadvantage. Her husband was of course included in the comparison.

She intimated her desire that her husband
should be more like her father. If her per-
sistent father-wishes irritated the casual visi-
tor, it was clear what their effect would be on
members of her household. Husband, mother-
in-law, and children were cowed by her constant father-eulogy. The purpose of the
husband in inviting me was soon confessed.
He wanted me to use my lecture to reveal to
his wife her selfish and childish attitude. The
wife was apparently suspicious of his desire
and gave one excuse after another for not going to the lecture. Finally she accidentally cut
her finger with a kitchen knife—with what
the Freudians would have called a subcon-
scious determination. Even this, however,
did not allow her to escape, for opportunity
was found for me to talk with her in private,
later, and to give her as much unwelcome
insight as she appeared likely to tolerate and
profit from. Whether this helped or not I do
not know, but speaking to her husband
strengthened his determination to harden himself against the expression of his wife's
tyranny.

I have known adults who have made it their

life purpose to prevent the growing up of a child.   In such cases the adult's selfishness is itself built upon an unwillingness to face life with maturity and sincerity.   Some twenty-five years ago a young girl only eighteen took over the management of a large family upon the death of her mother.   Lonely as a result of the household responsibilities she assumed with her sacrifice for family loyalty, she was easily exploited by a male friend of her father's, and gave birth to an illegitimate child which soon died, whereupon her emotions fixed themselves on her youngest brother. After a time these two were left together, all the other members of the family having died or left home.   For the last three or four years there has been constant difficulty between the brother and sister, the sister having an emotional upset of a very serious character if the brother pays any attention at all to other women.   She regards even the thought of marriage on his part as treason and a contemptuous disregard of her sacrifice.   As Fra Lippo Lippi found that he had sworn his life away for a taste of bread when he was a hungry lad, so it appears that when the brother in his helpless childhood accepted his sister's help he was supposedly making a contract to remain always a child, or from her viewpoint become a traitor in affection. The contract he simply cannot fulfill. He is too honest to conceal this fact. As a result his sister plays constantly upon his sympathies and by upbraiding him, shedding tears, and becoming sick tries to drive him back to childhood and a complete subserviency to her emotions.

We are all familiar with the common tendency of human nature when angry with someone from whom the emotion must be concealed to take it out on somebody else. It is not strange that children are often the victims of parents who immoderately scold or punish their offspring as a means of venting the anger or dissatisfaction they cannot safely show to the employer, customer, or rival who roused it. This situation is so commonplace that everybody knows it and takes it for granted. On the other hand, it is not so widely recognized that this same mechanism works with reference to other emotions. For example, anyone suffering from chronic feelings of inferiority will seek opportunities to show power just as one suffering a secret anger finds some substitute for an immediate expression of feeling.

The strict discipline of a parent who wants to show his authority in the home in order to gain relief from his inner sense of inferiority is not for the good of the child, but entirely for the parent's own personal satisfaction. Instead of benefiting from such discipline, the child reacts to it with antagonism because he is keen enough to interpret the real basis of his forced obedience.

Recently a young man came for advice with reference to an adjustment problem. His father has been a business man in a small way, and for some reason apparently has always had a strong feeling of social inequality. Meek on the outside, he has been a perfect tyrant at home. His two children have been brought up with exceptional severity; all their natural desires for self-expression have been thwarted. The father has dominated the home at every point and constantly intruded his authority into the affairs of his children. Under this home influence the son also has developed an excessive feeling of social inferiority. It was this that was making for him his problem of adjustment. As soon as the subject of his father came up, he gave way to an emotional upheaval that showed the nature of his difficulty. I had never before come in contact with such violent hatred of a parent. The young man frankly said that if the father died it would give him great pleasure. To quote his own words, 'If father died to-night, my only feeling would be one of intense relief. I would do nothing to bring about the event, but I should be most happy to have it happen.'

The more one has to do with problems of family life, the more one is impressed by the fact that so many difficulties are the result, not of lack of good will, or deliberate malice, but want of understanding. This does not seem so strange when one remembers how little attention is given to the preparing of human beings for parenthood. If an intelligent person starts even to keep hens, he usually buys some book to give him information. It is surely not easier to keep children than hens, but many a parent would feel you were criticizing him if you suggested that he needed to get information regarding the raising of children.

Fortunately it has become common for parents of an intelligent type to realize that they at least need books of instruction regarding the physical welfare of their very young children.   This is an advantage to the children and makes for better parenthood.   Excellent books have been provided by medical authorities, and they are widely sold and carefully read.   But the child is not all body; the other side of his personality is no easier to handle than his physical needs.   The value of books on child training is not only that they give important information, but also that they stimulate the thought of the parent and sharpen his attention with reference to the personality difficulties of the child.

In talking over child problems with parents I have found it effective when they have had experience with dogs to use the puppy as an illustration.   Anyone who has tried to train a dog realizes the significance of early happenings and how easily the animal can be hurt. It is well understood that any expression of anger, for example, may quickly spoil the puppy's disposition and ruin his training. When it is pointed out that this is equally true in the training of children, the comparison has force. Indeed, judging by the display of books on the training of dogs in the book-stores, there is a larger demand for books on the care of dogs than for books on child training. Apparently, many parents have greater confidence in their skill in dealing with their children than in their ability to train puppies. Actually, the child is a much more difficult proposition and can be more seriously hurt. Probably these parents believe that intuition—and by this they mean instinct—is a thoroughly satisfactory guide. Yet such instincts as we possess can have little real value in dealing with the complex problems that a modern parent has to face.

Other parents simply try to follow the methods of their own parents, or in some cases they feel that their parents have greatly failed with them and they take the opposite course. Either program runs the risk of not being at all adapted to the child in question. Social conditions have never so radically changed as they have during the last generation.

Consider how efficiently we furnish, heat, and light our homes as compared with thirty years ago. Even the cooking has changed as a result of better food preservation, standard preparations, quicker transportation of fruits and vegetables, and better knowledge of diet needs. The home in its inner life has changed fully as much as these externals, but tender memories of our childhood home experience cling to us, and the home as we construct it emotionally remains as it once was. We know changes are taking place—they are so obvious everyone realizes them—but we are apt to neglect them in dealing with home problems. And yet these changes cannot be ignored, for they are providing the actual home conditions which our children experience and to which they must adjust themselves.

The farmer's son to-day hurries through his work, jumps into the family car—or his own jazz contraption of cast-off parts—and scoots with his chum to a dance in the town or city anywhere from fifteen to fifty miles distant. Some sixteen-year-old boys and girls, in country or town, drive their own high-powered cars or have the parents' car always at their disposal, since the youths may be the only members of their respective families able and willing to drive.

The movies eat up the leisure, not only of the city children, but of those who live in once-lonely hamlets, far from village and railroad: if the city youngsters spend many hours a week idly watching the pictures that move, their cousins in the country spend a great deal of time talking and thinking of the pictures they have seen at the nearest movie-house, and traveling back and forth over the road from the farm to this outpost of modern city life.

Last year a New York City theatrical management broadcasted the announcement that positions were open for a number of chorus girls, previous experience and training entirely unnecessary. Girls of sixteen and seventeen, in city and hamlet, thrilled at this news, and a multitude of them applied for the places. Like the moving picture and the automobile, the radio has speeded up city life as it affects children and has done away with many of the differences between country and city environment.

The increasing number of mothers who

work outside the home, the lack of space for outdoor play, and the cramped quarters within doors in the ever more popular flat tend to make the childhood experiences of the growing boy and girl to-day very unlike the activities of Dad and Mother when they were young. This means of course, as everybody recognizes, that if we are to adapt ourselves to actual present conditions, we must have a home life which is different from that of our parents and very different from that of our grandparents.

Clearly as some see this with reference to most things, they fail utterly to realize that it is particularly true of the task of parenthood. Children are living in the world that now is and they must adjust themselves to it; the privilege of the parent is to help them make this necessary adjustment. To attempt to deal with them as children were dealt with a generation ago is a helpless undertaking, likely to bring disaster to the family. The wholesome parent has no choice: he must change his attention from his own childhood experiences to those his child is receiving.

No emotions are harder to control or mature

than those that distort the facts of everyday life by clinging to childhood experience. It is this that makes sentiment so treacherous, especially in the parent who can see his child only through lenses colored by an emotional recollection of his own early years. No amount of sentimental interpretation of the distant childhood provides the insight needed for dealing with the child of to-day.

Recently one of my students, a high-school teacher, investigated the attitudes of four classes of boys regarding the youth conditions of their fathers. This group, apparently representative of American youth, had absolutely no interest in or sympathy with the conditions under which their fathers were reared. Only four boys stated that they had any desire to do at all as their fathers did.

Doubtless these fathers often attempt to strengthen an argument with their boys or enforce advice by a reference to their own childhood experiences; they take it for granted that their sons share their feeling of reverence for those golden days. This appeal is the weakest possible, for the children are too busy dealing with the exacting present to have any real interest in conditions that seem as distant and stupid—shocking as it may seem to some parents, stupid exactly expresses the reaction of their youth—as the ox team.

In spite of the help the parent receives from such institutions as the church, the school, and other social-service organizations that have taken over responsibilities which once belonged exclusively to him, the parent's task is more difficult rather than easier. The demands placed upon the child have multiplied and his opportunities of failing have thereby increased. On the other hand, the quantity of responsibility that falls upon the parent has been lessened, while the significance of the influence that still remains to the home has to the same degree grown larger.

Psychology and sociology are constantly showing the social menace of parents who are emotionally immature and refuse to grow up, and are therefore utterly unfit to exercise the present responsibilities of parents. It is not surprising that some of the specialists—the social worker, the school official, and the church leader—are expressing a practical skepticism in regard to the possibility of developing wholesome parenthood and at every opening are trying to encroach on what was once parental responsibility.

If the modern parent is emotionally incapable of seeing his need of training, or if he is so selfish that he will not make the sacrifice and effort to train himself for his parenthood task, the trend of society will be unmistakably toward a smaller and smaller family responsibility, until the home, for all practical purposes, will be little more than a breeding place. Some are so doubtful of the family's doing wisely even under these circumstances that they hopefully look forward to the time when science will be able to propagate human life artificially and do away with the family altogether. It is hardly fair, however, to say that parents cannot be socially efficient until a genuine effort is made to help them meet their opportunities.

Those who have lost confidence in the family as a socially progressive institution and hold it to be at best but a necessary evil, whose mistakes other institutions must counteract, may well consider that parents are not the only adults who fail to grow up emotionally.

Teachers and social workers, and even court judges have been known to reveal infantile failings.

If the closeness of the family, its familiarity, and its freedom of emotional expression are the sources of its faults, here also is the explanation of its power. It is the most human of our institutions and, therefore, the best anchored in man's nature. What we need is better homes, rather than more or better substitutes for the home.

Better homes depend on better parents. It will prove more profitable for those interested in social progress to attempt to train parents to meet their obligations than to build up organizations to tempt parents to farm out still more of their old functions. If little effort is now being made to train parents, it is not because such training is unnecessary or impossible to obtain. Training for parenthood may sound new but it is perhaps older than history itself. At least we know that the savage, handicapped by his meagreness of knowledge, tried to give this training. Religion has usually included some degree of parenthood training in its program.

It is scientific training that parents have hitherto lacked, and that is just the training that can most help parents. We could not build a modern house without using constantly the findings of applied science. Why should we expect to establish a modern home on tradition rather than on science? What we need now is a wide understanding that parenthood has special difficulties because it permits adults to conceal infantile emotions which no other human relationship will allow. We must also admit the need of every parent's having the preparation for his life-task that science and only science can give.

Science has its morality and it is prepared to draw up for parents a code of conduct that will square the parents' influence with the child's needs:

Don't show off your child. It is not the duty of the child to feed a parent's vanity, but the parent's task to forget self-pride in dealing with his child.

Don't hurry your child. Adulthood is not a station toward which the child should be rushed, but a product of growth, and the growing process is the important thing.   You can't mold children: they have to grow.

Don't use your child as a means of ridding yourself of emotions that you dare not express to equals.

Don't expect commands to function in place of fellowship.   Children can be led but not driven in these days.

Don't lie to your child or permit anyone else to do so.   Your real opinions and beliefs may be far enough from the child's later judgment, but your deceit will be hopelessly distant. Sentiment easily leads to false statements.

Don't use fear as a whip.   Fear can only succeed by making slaves, and slaves, even when obedient, are poor substitutes for full human beings.

Don't stress the weaknesses of your child. He may take seriously what you point out to him and develop feelings of inferiority or he may glue his attention on your own weaknesses and lose respect for you as a harping hypocrite.

Don't tell your child that he cannot reason. He can and will if you have the wit to help him.

Don't let your home crowd out your child: put the child first and adjust home life to his needs.

Don't be a tyrant to your child even if you have power. Children are helpless and long suffering and usually generous in their judgment of parents. Nevertheless, a parent who drives his child from sheer love of dominance runs risk of soon losing the child's love. The child will some time be free, but the parent lonely.

The gist of it all is: Don't be emotionally childish if you desire manly and womanly children.

CHAPTER IX

THE FUTURE OF THE HOME

THE title of this chapter will carry an ominous suggestion to many a reader. There is a widespread practical skepticism regarding the future of the family. Nearly every day we hear somebody announce his conviction that the family is breaking down. Articles in newspapers and magazines express the opinion that things are not going well with the home; even in books we find dire prophecies regarding the modern home and its future prospects.

This popular doubt of the home is most certainly a modern characteristic. In the past there have been philosophical thinkers like Plato who have been dissatisfied with the prevailing form of family life and have suggested either radical changes or some sort of substitute for the conventional family.

The great mass of people have never before been touched by this questioning of the family. The stability of the family has been taken for granted with the same confidence that the law of gravitation has been assumed since its first discovery. The family has seemed a matter of fact, it has appeared so fundamental to life. There have always been criticisms of bad family life, but those who have pointed out the faults of the family have been the most certain of the absolute necessity of the right kind of home life and the most confident of the social security of the home.

The significance of the marked change in public attitude in recent years as shown in the everyday discussions of family problems is apparent to anybody who stops to consider what is behind such a radical veering of sentiment. Criticism of the family is becoming commonplace. To what extent this doubt of the home is based upon the personal experience of those who give voice to it we cannot know; nor can we discover how far criticism of the home is justified by actual results that come out of the family contacts, for it is impossible to tell how often the family is made a scapegoat for social conditions outside the household that are having a mischievous effect upon young life.

In any case we must accept the fact that the

future of the family is not as strongly established in the minds of modern men and women as was true in the thinking of even a decade ago. Things are certainly happening that are shaking the earlier complacency regarding family life. We are not so sure as once we were that the family can take care of itself; we hear much about the necessity of training parents; we see on every hand institutions and organizations that complain of family inefficiency and that in one way or another are attempting to do for children what once was the task of parents.

It is of course true that other institutions are receiving their share of criticism. Man is not as happy socially as he believes he has a right to be; he does not yet gain in happiness all that his magnificent conquest of nature appears to make possible. It is to be expected that the family, like other institutions, such as the church and the school, should come in for a critical examination. There is also a general tendency for those interested in any particular institution to cast blame upon the others for the obvious failures of social adjustment of modern youth.

Perhaps no topic of discussion brings out so tremendously personal prejudice as the home. Sentiment runs strongly with reference to family life, primarily because we are all saturated with the results of our own treatment in childhood. Not only do we generalize from our own experiences: we are all so powerfully in the grip of emotional reactions to the family life into which we were born and to the sort of home which fate has given us as adults that we cannot rid ourselves of personal bias when we begin to talk about family problems.

The strong current of sentiment that flows out of individual family experience, particularly as it issues from early childhood, sweeps aside calm judgment. Here is one of the handicaps of many modern parents: they cannot help their children make the necessary adjustments of contemporary life because they cling so tenaciously to the situations that were characteristic of their childhood environment. They readily see that other things should change; but although intellectually they admit the same fact regarding family life, when it comes to dealing with specific problems they find themselves instinctively assuming that the old ways were normal and that the difficulties that confront the youth of to-day are due to their having wandered away from the safe pathway and being out of harmony with the right sort of family life. This prejudice is of course a mischievous influence. Were it not for the natural sympathy of children with their parents and the recognition that their parents mean well, even though they see not clearly, the harmful results of such a situation would be greatly increased.

It follows, therefore, that even to ask the question whether the family has a future creates immediate hostility on the part of some who think such a question treason against human experience. On the other hand there are those who, coming out of an unhappy family life, enjoy making woeful prophecies concerning the passing of the home and the need of radically transforming marriage and what in the past has been the orthodox family way of living. A great multitude of people, however, are sane-minded when it comes to discussing the family: they see its faults; they are frightened by the rapid changes taking place within the family circle; they look back wistfully to the home of their childhood; but they are quite confident that human nature will cling to the family and will find a way to make it as large a contributor to human happiness as it has been in earlier times. Although they do not have misgivings regarding the future of the family they recognize that there is serious need of considering the plight of the modern family, which seems to be in the throes of adjustment to the new circumstances of our highly organized modern civilization. Such persons welcome a discussion of family tendencies, if only the analysis be impartial and conducted with scientific sincerity.

In a sense the future is always a closed book: we are of the present although we carry with us the records memory keeps for us of our past. We are always facing the future and walking toward it but by the time we have actually entered it, it is already the present; we therefore are never quite sure of what lies just before us as we travel onward, but usually if we try we can have some idea of general direction. A careful examination of the present pathway gives us a reasonable certainty as to what we are soon to encounter: it is only thus that we can judge of the future of the family; we must if possible discover the present trends that are appearing in family life and infer what they mean for us in the experiences just ahead.

In such an investigation we must beware of being deceived by special conditions that must not be taken so seriously as to cause a misinterpretation of the general tendencies of family life; it is also necessary for us not to think of the family as standing by itself, but as something which represents an interplay between the desires within its own four walls and the conditions outside and the effect of these conditions upon those who construct their personalities from influences born both of the outside and the home environment.

The modern family finds itself, as has been stated in an earlier chapter, in transition; we grant that the family always has been in the process of growth but the marked characteristics of our present family situation are that this transitional process has become so conscious and that we are passing through it so rapidly. It has become a trait of modern life to move fast and family changes are in accord with the general momentum. In these days we do not slide through our social difficulties entirely blinded; we have grown sensitive to social maladjustment; we are clearly aware of the fact that our troubles come out of our failures in human contact; we crave a new and better social existence because it has become imperative for human happiness that we should make greater progress in our social experiences.

We are not in a condition to make a comparison between the home of the past and that of the present: modern home life is better or worse according to the standards of life and the goals of human happiness that one assumes. What we do see clearly is that, whether the home has improved or not, it is not yet good enough to satisfy the needs of modern life. Change, therefore, it must; the force that drives it forward into new forms is the eternal yearning of the human spirit for a larger quantity of satisfactions.

There can be no doubt, therefore, that the family of the future must continue to change until it forms itself into an organization that more largely satisfies a greater number of people; it must learn to do more efficiently its human task. The social pressure bound to be put upon parents will call for a higher degree of skill and wiser judgment in dealing with the problems of children. When modern science, particularly psychiatric science, dug up and exposed to view the fact that the influences that determine the character of personality, so far as they are social in origin, come in the early years of childhood it was inevitable that a more serious attitude should follow concerning the obligations of parenthood. Science is bound to press this new understanding of the meaning of parenthood deeply into the social consciousness and there will be less and less opportunity for parents to hide behind the failures of other institutions in protecting themselves from social criticism because of the appearance of undesirable traits in their children.

The nursery school, rightly conducted, will relieve the parents of many of the concrete tasks that of necessity are performed by them at present, but it will most certainly also lift the plane of parenthood responsibilities and demand that fathers and mothers coöperate with it by treating the child while they have him with greater consideration and a much more skillful technique. The indifferent parent that encourages the nursery school movement with the expectation of getting rid of more responsibilities and winning a larger amount of leisure to be devoted to self-indulgence altogether misses the meaning of the new educational activity. The nursery school is bound not only to be a place where parenthood faults are corrected, but also a means of revealing the wrong practices of parents at so early a time in the life of the child that the parent has absolutely no excuse for fostering bad habits and unfortunate emotional trends. The parent cannot say that other institutions have spoiled the child because the child comes freshly from the home environment. The nursery school will relieve the parent, especially the mother, from doing as much for the child as has been customary in the past, but it will at the same time make greater demands in the way of character upon the fathers and mothers to whom it administers its service.

We have every reason to suppose that the future development of the family will mean a wider understanding of the significance of parenthood and that society will respond to this knowledge of the part that parents play in the formation of the character of their children by insisting that fathers and mothers meet their responsibilities with more conscious and more adequate preparation. The relation of parent and child will not be merely one of mutual responsibility, for the parent will be held more and more responsible to society itself and the mischievous effects of bad parenthood will be regarded not only as an injury of the child but even more as a blow against society itself.

The decreasing birth rate will also lend its influence in magnifying the responsibilities of parenthood. Even the valuing of children illustrates the significance of the law of supply and demand. Children grow cheap when they become over-abundant; it is equally true that a lowering of the birth rate increases the concern of social leadership that parents give to their children proper physical and social conditions.

It is likely, at least in the immediate future, that our birth rate will continue its decreasing trend. Particularly in the so-called working class are we likely to see a marked drop in the birth rate. It is to be hoped that the middle class will at any rate not go below its present reproductive record. We may be sure that children are not to be so cheap again because of a high birth rate as they have been in the past.

Even if the small family soon to be a recognized characteristic of the modern home should not lead to a heightened sensitiveness of parental attitude toward children, social pressure will most surely lay upon parents higher standards of responsibility in dealing with their children because child life will have arrived at a premium and social policy will register this fact.

When we admit, as we certainly must, that man's dominance, exercised for so many centuries in the past that it has appeared to be one of the unchanging fundamentals of human life, is passing we prophesy for some time to come a considerable disturbance in the inner life of families. It would be most unreasonable to suppose that men and women can easily adjust themselves to so marked a change in their social situations. There is bound to be for a while a testing experience for both men and women. At present the gulf between the two sexes is increasing because they sense so differently the new condition of affairs.

Woman realizes that at last her opportunity has come and she turns to it with avidity, at first assuming that man also understands how greatly woman's status has changed. When she discovers, as she often does, that man has little inkling of the seriousness of the change she either struggles to force herself back to the earlier situation of her mother, that she may the better conform to what is desired of her by man, or unconsciously she hides from the males in whose association fate throws her how radically she has departed from the social attitudes of the past, or she expresses herself without reference to man's reaction; often she wavers between these attitudes until she hardly knows whether she belongs to the old or the new. In any case her rôle is difficult, especially if she accepts a genuine share of family responsibility.

Man does not find his situation more comfortable although he has less idea as to what is the cause of his predicament. It is hard for him not to hamper woman's new freedom instinctively, even if his convictions are on the side of equal opportunity for women; social habits do not change easily; emotional attitudes are still more tenacious. It is almost impossible for the average man to realize that what woman wants is a life as free as his own. It may be that nature has denied this to her; her so-called biological handicap may be such as to make it absolutely impossible for her ever to reach the quantity of freedom enjoyed by man, but she at least will never be convinced of this by anything less than demonstration that comes from experience. The immediate future is to be the testing time. Woman will both claim and obtain all the equality that she craves until she herself is convinced, if actual experience should prove this true, that nature has dealt less generously with her and has put upon her a handicap she cannot shake off.

It will fall to the men of the generation now coming on to deal with women who are committed to an equality programme for their life. Not only do most men not see this with clearness, even though they recognize that there is something in women's desires that makes them less like their mothers than many men would like, but it must be confessed also that the deeper motives of men are out of sympathy with the radical change in woman's point of view. It would be strange if it were otherwise, since man's whole philosophy of life is permeated with influences that have come out of a previous subserviency of woman. Every aspect of family life, even where the utmost affection prevails, will be affected to some degree in the next few years by the new attitude of women that has become so widespread that no woman, however sheltered in childhood or isolated by living in a remote section, can escape having what some men would interpret as a sort of infection.

Woman signed her declaration of independence when first she obtained equal opportunity for education. It is indeed true, as Lester Ward has told us, that no large group can be kept in an inferior position unless they be restricted educationally. New knowledge means new cravings, new insight is followed by new demands, new achievements insist upon greater opportunities. Once woman began to get a chance for intellectual development, she rushed forward and soon was found in every part of the territory given over to the educational enterprise. She could not be driven back to her former subserviency; gradually she will push aside every artificial barrier. Man must accept her as she is or not at all. The only handicaps that in the long run can be placed upon her will be those established by nature, if such there are, for at present science is utterly unable to distinguish any from the artificial restrictions that have been imposed by social custom for so long a time.

Without question the family of the future will be a healthier and more wholesome family because both man and woman will press forward without limitations placed upon the growth of their personality by custom. Man in the end will like the new woman better, but it will not be strange if for a time he finds it something of a trial to bring himself into harmony with so radical a change of circumstances.

There is another social condition which means difficulty for the modern home. Human nature has at last planted itself upon a pleasure basis. Whether or not we have been able to work out a democracy of government or of cultural distribution, no one is likely to doubt that we have popularized the desire for luxury so that it has entered into every class of life. It is this democracy of desire that has the greatest significance in coloring the philosophy that now controls our practical living.

It is science, of course, that has performed the miracle; by its applications to industry it has made possible an enormous accumulation of things that have to do with the comforts and pleasures of life; it also has provided effective means by which human desires can be quickened and spread by the contagion made possible by modern forms of communication so that all normal youths conceive of life in terms of pleasure. At no point has the influence of the moving-picture been greater than in its spreading of the knowledge of luxury among those economically most unfortunate until they react with either hope or envy regarding the possessions that their predecessors assumed to be the exclusive right of the wealthy, granted by a fate that expressed the divine ordering of the affairs of the world. Now there is no class barrier to desire: if one can not have, one can at least daydream about what one thinks of as belonging to the normal type of life.

Such a change will be sure to influence family life. Indeed, it is clear now that the family is responding to a democratic interpretation of pleasure, so far as the delay of marriage is concerned. The middle class, as one would expect, is gathering the first fruits of this change. It is natural to expect, however, that the new conception of life will eventually affect somewhat the so-called working class, particularly that portion which is emerging into the middle class or has already arrived, as far as the comforts of life are concerned.

It is not merely in later marriage or a decreasing birth rate that we expect to find the effect of the new popularizing of luxury; the success of family life itself will, to a large degree, be interpreted in terms of pleasurable experiences. The founding of family life will be considered a luxury that must win its existence in competition with other desires more difficult to obtain if the family be maintained.

We shall find higher standards demanded of marriage experience. Nothing is likely to decrease the tendency toward divorces except some way by which married life will become a greater source of happiness than it now is for a multitude. Marriage will itself be scrutinized and judged a success by its ability to provide a larger quantity of pleasure. This is a more exacting requirement than one might suppose when one remembers that those who enter married life, because they have been committed so thoroughly to the pleasure philosophy of life, will be more reluctant to accept the necessary checks on personal attainment that always follow when two individuals try to live together. We may exaggerate this trend in modern life and forget the neutralizing motives born of affection and notably of parenthood that lead to sacrifice and self-denial.

The movement is unmistakable: human nature more and more expects of marriage satisfactions that can be catalogued under the concept of pleasure. It is easy for true values to be concealed when from every quarter come clamoring voices that seek to advertise the importance of every conceivable type of enjoyable activity. The newly established family is from its beginning weighed down by the load of pleasurable expectations heaped upon it. It is difficult for the home to develop character when it is assumed to be so largely a pleasure-furnishing enterprise.

For the present we must therefore expect a high percentage of marriage failures. Divorces are primarily a statement of home failure; whatever their special cause in definite instances, they represent as a whole the inability of the two persons concerned to live happily together; they announce to all observers the large place that happiness holds in the substance of family organization.

It is folly to turn to outside pressure as a means of protecting the family from breakdowns that signify the failure of the individuals to be happy in their association. Men and women enter marriage, not only confident that they are to be happy, but insistent that they have what they anticipated. Usually they want quick results and when unforeseen obligations appear they resent these intruding duties and treat them as if they were evidences of a social deceit that had been practised upon the young lovers. Frequently a divorce is not evidence of an incompatibility, but rather of impatience. People who have signed up to a pleasure philosophy of life are not likely to be patient when their desires are curbed by unexpected obstacles that have been concealed in what they supposed were prize packages filled with pleasure.

Nevertheless, it is fortunate that family life must increasingly depend upon its inner vitality. Men and women marry to be happy and they are less likely to continue living together when they have lost their hope of happiness than was the case with their fathers and mothers, who had a larger sense of social responsibility and a more reasonable expectation regarding the attainment of pleasure.

The lesson for those who are concerned for the welfare of the home is that we must make ever greater use of science in our education to prepare people to live happily together in marriage. Everybody acquainted with the practical problems of married life is convinced that much of the difficulty that snatches happiness from those who confidently look forward to it is lack of preparation for marriage itself. People enter marriage with too much ignorance as well as too great demands. Other relationships, to be successful, require preparation. Those who enter marriage also have the right to expect of society that they be given all available information to make their adventure a satisfying experience. Society is naturally so set in its old habits that it would probably not be much concerned about educating for marriage, were it not for the pressure exerted upon it by the ever-increasing divorce rate.

We have no reason to suppose that the tendency so clearly manifest at present to have the home pass over more and more of its functions to organizations that are ambitious to do things that formerly were done by the home, and well-prepared to do them efficiently, will decrease. It is doubtful whether this current has yet reached its maximum. Such a division of labor is inevitable with the development of a civilization so complicated as ours and so thoroughly urban in its point of view. The rural family will continue in large measure to perform its present function so far as children are concerned. The city family, however, will be more representative of the type of family adapted to our present-day culture. The tendency to remove from the family functions that once it had is not something new; it has been going on ever since the Industrial Revolution. Now we have the stripping process carried farther and expressing itself in taking from the family functions that for so long a time have been part of the home programme that it seems as if the family were losing its essential qualities.

The test is not what other institutions would like to take from the family, or what the family would prefer to keep, or what shiftless parents are eager to pass over to outside organizations in order that they themselves may be to that extent freed from irksome responsibilities; the only question at issue is what ought the family to keep in order to be well adapted to do its part in the training of children? If it tries to keep to itself trivial functions or if it seeks to hold what other organizations are better fitted to do, its policy is hostile to progress. Perhaps nothing but experience can reveal with certainty how many of its old tasks the family can give up for the good of the child. In a test where so many complications are present and where it is so difficult to separate the part that any one institution contributes in the growth of a child's personality, we can not quickly or easily come to any conclusion, but in the long run experience is surely going to demonstrate what the family ought to do and what it ought not to do in the bringing up of its own children.

The nursery school is the most aggressive attack yet made on the conventional programme of family policy. Thus far it appears to be proving itself by actual service which convinces parents that it performs for children a function that the home cannot so adequately carry out; it has come, naturally, first in the city and flourishes for the most part in our large centres, at least as far as this country is concerned. It has had a longer English history, but on the other side its programme is more in harmony with former practices than in America, for the English boarding-school has always had a large place in private education and it has taken children at a younger age than has been common in similar schools in the United States. Although the nursery school thrives best in the city thus far, we have at least one school of this sort in a small village. It is because of its unique character that there is such a general interest among those engaged in this movement in Mrs. Schofield's nursery school at Peterborough, New Hampshire. The Peterborough demonstration may reveal that the nursery school is just as much needed and can be just as successful in the village or town as in the city. The expense of maintaining this kind of school and the more conservative attitude of people living outside the cities will, however, for a time restrict it mostly to the larger places.

Friends of the family who have great confidence in its power to serve human need must constantly keep in mind that it is not a question of what the home can do, but of what it ought to do. When we apply this test there can be little doubt that we find a constant trend toward a decreasing function on the part of the home. What has been happening during the last decade will undoubtedly continue and this tendency may become even more pronounced. It would be a misinterpretation of this current to assume that it means dissolving the family little by little until it has so small a place in modern social life that aside from biological necessity it will seem superfluous.

It is true that those who doubt the power of the family to meet the competition of other institutions, assuming that the family can not be vital unless it engages in a quantity of activities for the child, forget that the security of the home in the future is not to depend upon how much it does, but rather upon how well it does the things that it alone should do. The question at issue can not be decided by prejudice, but by actual experience. Meanwhile, the way to help the family is not to protect it from outside competition, so much as to increase its efficiency and strengthen its good purposes. The right sort of family does not look into the future with misgivings, fearful that it will be left without purpose because it has for the greater welfare of the child turned over some of its former activities to organizations founded to perform specialized tasks.

In recent years a rival of the orthodox family has appeared in what is well termed the *companionate*. This is the marriage of a man and woman who have agreed to avoid the having of children. It is a new kind of marriage that could not have arisen, were there not such widespread confidence that those who so desire can escape, even though married, the coming of children.

Many companionates are merely temporary in character, at least so far as the plans of husband and wife go. They do not mean never to have children, but only to wait until they are ready and the birth of a child will not hamper their ambitions or limit their pleasures. Needless to say, their designs do not always work out as they expect. For some the situation which would make a child desirable never arrives. They postpone and postpone until at length they find their companionate made permanent by their growth in years. Others, still young, finally decide that the time has at last come when without risk to their professional or social ambitions they can indulge in a child, only to discover that nature has not been coöperating with them in their planning and that their companionate must continue, enforced by a sterility that is no longer in their control.

The great majority of the companionate matings are from the first attempts at permanent childlessness, and although some of them are turned into families by the appearance of an unwanted child, most of these marriages continue as they started. Companionship and intimate affection are craved but there is no intention of accepting the social obligations of a marriage that leads into parenthood.

The conditions of modern life are leading *companionators* to believe that their selection of a restricted kind of family life is the happiest solution of conflicting desires. Doubtless in all past times some couples have at heart preferred to remain childless and had opportunity been given them they would have formed companionates centuries ago. To-day, however, there are marked trends in our social life that would automatically encourage the companionate.

The popularity of our pleasure-philosophy, which has already been discussed, naturally leads people to avoid children. The child means expense and responsibility, how much cost and how great an obligation one can not calculate in advance. Personal comforts, freedom and luxuries are for many endangered by a child, who, once having appeared, cannot be got rid of if at any time his birth seems to have occasioned too heavy demands in care and sacrifice for the parents to be well-satisfied with their decision to accept a complete family life.

To call the attention of those who are committed to a companionate programme to the joys of parenthood is futile. For them the possibility of being driven out of the limited marriage experience they desire by the accidental coming of a child is a veritable nightmare. They feel no appeal in the enthusiasm of others who have and desire children, but are relieved that the continuation of society is so well established that there is little danger that social pressure will attack them and make them uncomfortable. It is indeed true that a large number of those who are forced from their companionate by unwilling parenthood discover that their affection for the child, once he comes, is just as strong as was that of their parents for them. This fact, although it reveals how little human impulses change, does not help to strengthen the orthodox type of family, since this experience is unconvincing to those who have not had it. If the time is near at hand, as some specialists think, when accidental pregnancy will be rare, so that those who prefer the companionate will be secure in their choice, the old-time family will not win recruits from those who have experienced the miracle nature has for so long been performing for reluctant parents by snatching away their self-centred purposes and giving them in return a taste of the joys of loving their own child.

So much of modern life is coaxing young married couples to avoid children that it is hard to say what influences deserve to be specially indicted. Certainly, love of luxury, our present stress of self-expression, and the intensity of competition are outstanding factors. On the other hand, the determination not to fall below one's present standards of living, the unwillingness to have children that one cannot care for and provide with the advantages that appear necessary to those who regard parenthood conscientiously are likewise influencing people to accept the companionate for motives that can not justly be called selfish.

The rapid growth of cities and the even greater extension of urban culture through the land tend to make the companionate desirable. The child in the city is a problem. In the semi-city life of the suburb he is only a little less a problem. Children need the open.

Our urban centers could, if they so desired, make the life of children safer and more normal than at present. They have, in fact, already accomplished wonders in lowering the death rate of infants. For the city parent, however, the child creates difficulties that the rural parent never experiences. For example, the city landlord who is just as willing to rent his apartments to families including young children as to childless couples is a rarity.

The city does not influence the companionate merely by making awkward problems for the parents; city life, just like intense intellectual competition, lessens fertility and in many cases brings about a proportion of companionates based on enforced sterility. The city also still spreads venereal disease more than rural and town communities, and this also decreases fertility.

The factors that are furthering the popularity of the companionate are not likely to pass or change greatly in the years just ahead. We can not expect in the near future a smaller

percentage of marriages that are companionate in type. The remote future is too far from
us to allow any prophecy. The companionate
is with us to stay. It will compete for favor
with the orthodox family. Its popularity will
increase or decrease according to the conditions of social life that prevail.

It may turn out well for the historic type
of family that it has so aggressive a rival.
Perhaps its need will be more clearly recognized, its handicaps removed as much as possible by education and legislation and customs that try to minister to family welfare.
Everything depends upon how clearly social
leadership will see the burdens of the present-
day home, the false values of mass judgments,
and the necessity of training for marriage and
parenthood. The home has been too much
taken for granted in our thinking. A social
situation has arisen which to a large degree is
undermining the fully developed form of marriage. Until these social conditions fundamentally change, the companionate will hold
its present popularity. Our present social situation can not be put into new forms quickly
in any case and as a consequence we shall in

the future that lies just ahead have both the family and the companionate contending for popular favor.

THE END